Light
for the
LAST DAYS

Jesus' End-time Prophecies Made Plain
in the Book of Revelation

Hans K. La Rondelle

Pacific Press® Publishing Association
Nampa, Idaho
Oshawa, Ontario, Canada

Edited by David C. Jarnes
Designed by Tim Larson
Cover photo by Richard Kaylin © Tony Stone

Copyright © 1999 by

Pacific Press® Publishing Association
Printed in the United States of America
All Rights Reserved

Library of Congress Cataloging-in-Publication Data

LaRondelle, Hans K.
   Light for the last days: Jesus' endtime prophecies made plain in the book of
Revelation
   / Hans K. LaRondelle.
      p. cm.
   Includes bibliographical references.
   ISBN 0-8163-1758-5 (pbk.)
   1. Bible. N.T. Revelation—Criticism, interpretation, etc. I. Title.

BS2825.2 .L277 2000   228'.06—dc21   99-057497

99 00 01 02 03 ● 5 4 3 2 1

Contents

"Dr. Hans LaRondelle has made a very valuable contribution to the understanding of biblical prophecy. Central to that understanding is a clear vision of the unity of apocalyptic prophecy, beginning with Daniel, running through the teachings of Jesus and Paul, and climaxing in the book of Revelation."

George R. Knight
Professor of Church History
Seventh-day Adventist Theological Seminary
Andrews University
Berrien Springs, Michigan, U.S.A.

"We live in an age when exciting breakthroughs are being made in many areas of knowledge. Not only can this be said of the sciences and history; it can also be said of our understanding of the Bible. However, most of this new information is hidden away in scholarly journals and books.

"As one who has kept abreast of the latest research, Dr. LaRondelle has written this book for the lay person or pastor who wishes to go deeper into a study of the last book in the Bible. He makes it possible for all to gain from the fresh insights that are now available.

"Starting with the premise that Christ's sermon on the end of the world as recorded in Matthew 24 is the seedbed for the book of Revelation, he develops his material in a way that enables the average reader to grasp the deeper meanings and insights. Of particular interest is the way in which he aligns the seals, the trumpets, and the plagues and shows their end-time messages."

Graeme S. Bradford
Ministerial Director
Trans-Tasman Union Conference
of the Seventh-day Adventist Church
Gordon, New South Wales, Australia

Foreword

As the thought of beginning a new millennium captures our imaginations, many wonder what the future holds. They also wonder what the Bible says about the end time and the purpose of human history. The authors of the Bible recorded their visions about the future in a prophetic language that needs interpretation today. There is a wide gap between their time, place, culture, and language, and those of our Western civilization. This gap must be bridged by a responsible method of interpretation and application to our modern world situation. The author of this book intends to help in bridging that gap.

To do so, to find this method of interpretation, we must understand particularly the relationship between the Old and the New Testaments of the Bible and between Israel and the church. This, in turn, requires a grasp of the larger picture of the prophetic portrayals in both Testaments. Especially important is the decisive influence of Jesus Christ on the understanding of the messianic prophecies—a task that continues to occupy professional theologians.

This author has devoted his professional life to increasing our understanding of the biblical prophecies and of the hope they offer us. The results of his studies have been published in various scholarly books: *The Israel of God in Prophecy: Principles of Prophetic Interpretation*, Andrews University Monographs, Studies in Religion,

Vol. 13 (Berrien Springs, Mich.: Andrews University Press, 1997); *Chariots of Salvation: The Biblical Drama of Armageddon* (Hagerstown, Md.: Review and Herald, 1987); and *How to Understand the End-Time Prophecies of the Bible: The Biblical-Contextual Approach* (Sarasota, Fla.: First Impressions, 1997).

The author wrote this book to make his findings accessible to everyone who wants a basic understanding of Bible prophecies. Avoiding theological debates, it presents the essence of the biblical prophecies in simple and plain language—beginning with a brief overview of Jesus' prophetic speech in Matthew 24 and of Paul's forecast of the Church Age in 2 Thessalonians 2 (background that helps us to understand the book of Revelation with its symphony of images and symbols).

Most intriguing is the discovery that John's Apocalypse conveys a narrative that *moves forward in history*, a movement that proceeds from promises to the seven churches in the first chapters to their fulfillment in the last visions of the book. So, rather than becoming outdated, this pastoral-prophetic letter becomes more timely as the years go by. Its focus sharpens increasingly on the time of the end— a movement that propels John's Apocalypse to the forefront of relevance for our time and age.

May this effort to share Revelation's significance benefit all seekers after truth and impart hope for the future to those who want to understand the meaning of it all.

Chapter One

THE ESSENCE
OF JESUS'
PROPHETIC TEACHING

To understand the book of Revelation, we must learn the essence of Jesus' prophetic teaching as recorded in the Gospels of Matthew (chapter 24), Mark (chapter 13), and Luke (chapter 21). John structured his book on this discourse. In fact, Revelation takes Jesus' prophecy of coming events and develops it in the light of His death and resurrection. This means that we must know the truth of the gospel Jesus taught before we can appreciate Revelation's portrayals of His present and future ministry.

While the Gospel writers focus their attention on the first coming of the Messiah and end their narratives with Jesus' crucifixion and resurrection, John's Apocalypse begins with the *risen* Christ and centers in His present rule and second coming. This focus makes the Apocalypse the complement of the four Gospels. Consequently, the significance of John's message in Revelation depends entirely on the truthfulness of the gospel message. The "wrath of the Lamb" and the Second Advent receive their full meaning only in the light of Jesus' first advent as God's visitation to humankind.

Jesus announced that He had been sent from heaven to reveal God's redemptive will through His life and teachings (John 12:49, 50). His presence radiated the saving power of God's kingdom among the Jews. As the promised Messiah, He claimed to fulfill the Hebrew Scriptures and their messianic prophecies. To the surprise of the rabbis, Jesus taught that the Hebrew Bible was not primarily Israel-centered but Messiah-centered. He declared: " 'You diligently study the Scriptures because you think that by them you possess eternal life. These are the Scriptures that testify about me, yet you refuse to come to me to have life' " (John 5:39, 40).

Jesus presented Himself as the great Reality to which the symbolic rituals and prophetic types of Israel's temple services pointed. He claimed to have been sent as the promised Lamb, Priest, Prophet, and King, all in one Person (see Matt. 12:6, 41, 42; Mark 10:45). With these messianic claims, Jesus presented Himself as the God-sent King for Israel and all people—as the true representative of the kingdom of God: " 'For, in fact, the kingdom of God is among you' " (see Luke 17:21, NRSV).

The Disciples' Double Question

We'll focus on Matthew 24 because this passage presents the most extensive record of Jesus' prophetic speech and directly establishes its essential continuity with Daniel (see v. 15). Jesus' prophetic outlook was deeply influenced by the apocalyptic book of Daniel, which He urged His followers to study and to understand (see Matt. 24:15). In fact, some scholars call His Matthew 24 discourse His *midrash,* or "commentary," on Daniel. Jesus adopted from Daniel the key terms He used—"kingdom of God," "Son of Man," "clouds of heaven," "desolating sacrilege," "the end," and "time of distress." And Daniel's prediction of the destruction of the second temple stands at the center of Jesus' discourse (Matt. 24:15-20; Dan. 9:26, 27). Consequently, we must understand His statements in Matthew 24 against the background of Daniel's outline of salvation history. (Revelation, then, goes on to develop Jesus' application of Daniel's unique outline of salvation history through the Christian age.)

Jesus' prophetic discourse was occasioned by His disciples' inquiry about the "sign" of the destruction of the temple and of His coming at the end of the world (Matt. 24:3). They assumed that both events would occur at the same time. Jesus didn't answer their twofold question by pointing out that the two events would take place at different times. Instead, He explained how His disciples could be prepared for both events and thus save their souls. Jesus didn't offer, in this "sermon," a chronological timetable of all future events. Rather, moved with pastoral concern for the salvation of His disciples, He warned them about the dangers of deceptions and persecutions that might distract them from persevering till the end. In this discourse, Jesus did not provide any specific order of events except to distinguish sharply between the fall of Jerusalem during the contemporary generation and His glorious *parousia* (or "appearance"; i.e., His second coming) in the unknown future (24:34, 36). For each of these events He mentioned a specific *sign* of its immediate occurrence.

The structure of Jesus' discourse resembles that of the discourses of the Hebrew prophets. This structure is called the "prophetic perspective" or "prophetic foreshortening" or the *typological perspective*. It consists of two parts: an imminent judgment in salvation history and the universal Judgment at the end of the world, the former being placed against the background of the latter. Israel's prophets customarily used this structure in their judgment oracles. The local judgment served as a warning "type," or model, of the world Judgment by the same Judge. So, for instance, Isaiah 13:4-8, 14-22 deals with the imminent fall of Babylon, while verses 9-13 look forward to the end-time judgment. Isaiah 34 and 63, which concern Edom, another archenemy of the Israel of God, are also built on this typological structure. Some have compared this perspective with a painting of several mountains in which peaks that are far removed from each other are portrayed as if they stand close together. "Such prophetic foreshortening is characteristic of the Old Testament prophets."[1] Similarly, Jesus made the imminent judgment on Jerusalem a type of the Judgment at His second coming. This is the interpretative key to understanding the basic structure of Matthew 24.

Jesus' reply to His disciples shows that the chronological distance between the two judgments was not His primary concern, just as it had no part in the messages of the Hebrew prophets. Both judgments come for the same reasons: the rejection of Christ as the God-sent Messiah and the persecution of His followers. So Jesus directed all attention to our present duty of returning to God in sincere repentance, of walking with Him and following His Messiah, whom He sent for humanity's redemption. The gospel and its sacred claims on us remain the guiding motif in Matthew 24. Jesus emphasized this by saying " 'he who stands firm to the end will be saved. And this gospel of the kingdom will be preached in the whole world as a testimony to all nations, and then the end will come' " (Matt. 24:13, 14). His words reveal His pastoral concern. They also constitute His commission to the church (see also 28:18, 20)! Note that He did not place this commission in the framework of the popular nationalistic expectations or of the apocalyptic timetables of late Judaism.

Jesus chose to use repetition in presenting His answer to the disciples. Here we see another resemblance to Daniel's book, in which the visions parallel each other (cp. chapters 2 and 7). Jesus gave two parallel summaries of the Christian age, the second of which directly answers the two questions of the disciples (see Matt. 24:15-31). Both summaries conclude with the end of the world (see 24:14, 30, 31). So, in Matthew 24, Jesus combined the typological perspective of the classical prophets with Daniel's style of parallel visions. The double focus of the questions of Jesus' disciples determines the basic structure of Matthew 24—raising the matters, first, of Jerusalem's doom in Jesus' own generation, and second, of the end-time generation that will see the sign of His glorious return.

Jesus' Prophetic Discourse

In His preliminary review of the church age (Matt. 24:4-14), Jesus enumerated first those events that should *not* be considered signs of the destruction of Jerusalem or of His imminent return: false messiahs, wars, famines, pestilences, and earthquakes in various places (24:4-8; Luke 21:8-11). Jesus did not place these events in any chronological order or make them part of any timetable. Such upheavals in society are not signs that the end is imminent or the Parousia near. They are, rather, signs of the age; they characterize the *entire* period between Jesus' two advents. Jesus explicitly warned against those who cry prematurely: " 'The time is near' " (Luke 21:8)! He explained that disasters in nature and society " 'are the beginning of birth pains' " (Matt. 24:8) and that " 'these things must happen first, but the end will not come right away' " (Luke 21:9). Jesus knew Daniel's warning that many wars and religious conflicts would occur before the end (see Dan. 11:11-13, 29-45). Paul said the same thing another way: "We know that the whole creation has been groaning as in the pains of childbirth right up to the present time" (Rom. 8:22).

What then was the point of Jesus' mentioning such recurring events? One Adventist scholar concludes that when disasters become increasingly intense, these signs are "designed to discourage date-setting sensationalism and to encourage believers throughout Christian history to look forward to the final consummation of redemption to be accomplished by the coming of the Lord."[2] Another explains:

"The pattern of Matthew 24 appears to be that the real signs are not signs of nearness but signs of coming. The less precise signs are to encourage believers to keep watching, waiting, and working."[3]

Jesus proceeded to mention the development of internal *apostasy and persecution* among His followers of "all nations" and the appearance of *false prophets* (Matt. 24:9-12) as characteristics of the entire church age. The book of Daniel repeatedly predicted that God's people would experience apostasy or a falling away from the true faith (see chapters 7–11), and we should understand Jesus' warnings in this light.

The book of Acts describes the initial persecution of the apostolic church by the Jewish leaders and the Sanhedrin (see Acts 4–9). Church history describes the persecutions conducted by the Roman Empire until the conversion of Emperor Constantine around A.D. 313. Soon afterwards the state church began persecutions that intensified during the dark Middle Ages, in fulfillment of Daniel 7:25. And Daniel ends with the prediction of a final, worldwide attack on the people of God that will be so intense that without divine intervention every believer would be killed (see Dan. 12:1, 2).

Jesus did not tie His prediction of persecution to any particular time period. Instead, He stressed His followers' responsibility to persevere till the end (Matt. 24:13). So, Matthew 24:4-14 contains Jesus' general overview or summary of the dangers and threats His followers would meet while they were fulfilling His commission of proclaiming the good news of the kingdom of God till the end of the age (Matt. 24:14).

So, Jesus first completed His call to faithfulness despite the troubles that He warned would come. Only then did He begin to answer directly His disciples' questions regarding the sign of the destruction of Jerusalem and that of the nearness of His parousia (Matt. 24:15-31). He began by mentioning one specific sign that would signal the imminent destruction of Jerusalem. He gave this sign—the sacrilegious desolator standing on the holy ground (24:15)—so that His disciples could flee from the doomed city in time. The fulfillment of this prediction came in Jesus' own generation, when the Roman armies came twice during the years A.D. 66-70 to subjugate the rebellious city to Roman rule, as Josephus reported in his *Wars of the Jews*.[4]

Luke's narrative fits perfectly the first approach of the Roman legions, in A.D. 66:

> When you see Jerusalem being surrounded by armies, you will know that its desolation is near. Then let those who are in Judea flee to the mountains, let those in the city get out, and let those in the country not enter the city (Luke 21:20, 21).

Christ warned His disciples: " 'I tell you the truth, all this will come upon this generation' " (Matt. 23:36). He urged them to flee to the mountains as soon as they saw the predicted sign. Fortunately, the Christian believers were alert to the sign and fled in time, saving their lives, as Eusebius noted.[5] Their prayers were answered, and the Christian community escaped destruction. In contrast, "a great number of false prophets" arose in the beleaguered city who promised that God would send "miraculous signs of their deliverance" if the citizens would stay in the city.[6] All who followed these deceivers lost their lives in the terrible slaughter. Thus the pastoral purpose of Jesus' predictions becomes evident.*

Unequaled Distress

Before answering His disciples' question regarding the sign of His parousia (Matt. 24:3), Jesus warned of an unprecedented time of "distress" (v. 21) (Greek: *thlipsis*—"distress, tribulation, affliction, trouble") that would come to those of His people who would see the sign of His parousia. He wasn't speaking of the general afflictions caused by wars and natural disasters but of a specific persecution of His faithful ones in the end time, as Daniel had foretold (Dan. 12:1):

> For then there will be great distress, unequaled from the beginning of the world until now—and never to be equaled again. If those days had not been cut short, no one would survive, but for the sake of the elect those days will be shortened (Matt. 24:21, 22).

The disciples had asked about the sign of the fall of Jerusalem and of Jesus' second coming. Jesus had answered the first question with sufficient clarity (Matt. 24:15-20; Luke 21:20, 21). He then concentrated fully on the final generation of His followers without explaining the chronological distance between the two events. He began by

---

*Significant also was Jesus' advice that His followers should start praying right away that " 'their flight will not take place in winter or on the Sabbath' " (Matt. 24:20). This pastoral concern indicates His intention that His followers should still be keeping the Sabbath forty years after His resurrection—not in the sense of a legalistic righteousness, "but in the way Christ kept the Sabbath" (Ed. Schweizer, *Matthäus*, NTD 2, 1973, 295; my own translation). A "flight on the sabbath would make any sabbath observance impossible" (D. A. Hagner, *Matthew 14-28*, Word Bible Commentary, 33B [Dallas: Word Books, 1995], 702).

stressing that His people will experience an "unequaled distress," one that would be of such a severe and global nature that He planned to intervene dramatically on their behalf: " 'If the Lord had not cut short those days, no one would survive. But for the sake of the elect, whom he has chosen, he has shortened them' " (Mark 13:20).

To understand this comforting promise that Jesus has made to the last generation, we must first determine its connection with the book of Daniel and then discover how the book of Revelation develops it. Daniel helps us here. He predicted two specific periods of persecution of the saints: one applicable to the Christian age (chapter 7:25), and the other involving the last generation of saints in "the time of the end" (chapter 12:1; see the context: 11:40-45). There can be no doubt that Jesus focused particularly on Daniel 12:1's final generation in His answer to His disciples' question about the sign of His second coming (see Matt. 24:3). A close comparison of Jesus' words with Daniel 12:1 reveals His unmistakable end-time focus (see the italicized words):

Daniel 12:1, 2	Matthew 24:21, 22
"At that time Michael, the great prince who protects your people, will arise. There will be *a time of distress* [Greek: *thlipsis*] *such as has not happened from the beginning of nations until then. But at that time your people—everyone whose name is found written in the book—will be delivered.* Multitudes who sleep in the dust of the earth will awake: some to everlasting life, others to shame and everlasting contempt."	"Then there will be great distress [Greek: *thlipsis*], *unequaled from the beginning of the world until now—and never to be equaled again.* If those days had not been cut short, no one would survive, but for the sake of the elect those days will be shortened."

It is crucial to remember that Daniel was describing here "the time of the end" in which the "king of the North" will invade the territory of God's people and prepare for his final attack against the saints "at the beautiful holy mountain" or Mount Zion (Dan. 11:40-

45). That final persecution will cause the unparalleled distress, or "great suffering," of the "elect" (Matt. 24:21, 22, NRSV) from which the heavenly Michael will suddenly deliver them by His divine intervention. Then the king of the North "will come to his end," and the dead will be raised (Dan. 11:45; 12:1, 2). This high point of all salvation history was in Jesus' mind when He answered His disciples' ultimate question, the one about His parousia. His quotation of Daniel 12:1 makes this evident. Not surprisingly, all professional exegetes acknowledge this view.

So, "those days" of great suffering and affliction mentioned in Matthew 24:21, 22 don't refer exclusively to the 1,260 years of Daniel 7:25. They include as well the worldwide tribulation of the final generation prophesied in Daniel 11:45; 12:1. Nor does "the elect" refer to the Jewish tribes. Instead, it denotes "his elect"—that is, all who belong to Jesus and are waiting for His second coming (Matt. 24:22, 24, 31). Daniel 12:1, then, contains the key to properly understanding Jesus' promise that the Lord will shorten those days of distress for the sake of His elect. Jesus endorsed this method of interpretation when He urged His disciples to study Daniel carefully (Matt. 24:15)! Consequently, this interpretation of this part of Matthew 24 takes precedence over one that makes an exclusive application to the Middle Ages—an interpretation that can provide only gradual and partial fulfillments in Europe, not the global deliverance of all the saints by one act of the divine Warrior.

The end-time distress differs in quality from the persecutions of previous times because only for the last generation of saints will God intervene on a global scale and suddenly end the affliction.[7] Jesus pointed specifically to Daniel 12:1 when He predicted that God Himself will cut short the unequaled, global distress. Jesus' promise of a supernatural deliverance at the end of the age is a wonderful consolation intended to encourage His followers to persevere till the end.

The Specific Sign of Jesus' Parousia

Having encouraged His people to remain faithful till the end in the face of apostasy, false christs, and false prophets with their deceptive miracles and persecution (Matt. 24:21-28), Jesus finally answers the question about the sign of His parousia:

> "Immediately after the distress of those days 'the sun will be darkened, and the moon will not give its light; the stars will fall from the sky, and the heavenly bodies will be shaken.' At that time [Greek: *tote,* "then"] *the sign of the Son of Man will appear in the sky, and* [*tote,* "then,"] *all the nations of the earth will mourn. They will see the Son of Man coming on the clouds of the sky, with power and great glory"* (Matt. 24:29, 30).

Jesus taught His disciples to look for one specific sign of the parousia of the Son of Man. This sign is not the eclipsing of the sun, moon, and stars, but the coming of the Son of Man "on the clouds of the sky" (Matt. 24:30). This is what Jesus said, and we must regard it with great seriousness!

This "sign of the Son of Man" that Jesus mentions in answer to His disciples' question is so overwhelming in its visible manifestation of Jesus' divine glory that "all the nations of the earth will mourn"—that is, all will be struck with remorse and fear. The book of Revelation describes the same global impact of Jesus' return:

> He is coming with the clouds, and every eye will see him, even those who pierced him; and all peoples [Greek: *phylai,* "tribes"] of the earth will mourn because of him. So shall it be! Amen (Rev. 1:7).

This announcement at the beginning of the Apocalypse links John's book with Jesus' prophecy in Matthew 24. Revelation 1:7 summarizes Matthew 24:30! We will discover that the Apocalypse is a development and clarification of Matthew 24. For instance, Revelation 6 explains why " 'all the nations of the earth will mourn' " (Matt. 24:30). It says all people will experience cosmic upheavals, picturing the sign of the Son of Man (Rev. 6:12-17). In that chapter we learn that the "mourning" is not true repentance but the mourning of the unsaved on the Day of Judgment. The sixth seal describes the universal impact of the shaking of heaven and earth:

> The kings of the earth, the princes, the generals, the rich, the mighty, and every slave and every free man hid in caves and among the rocks of the mountains. They called to the mountains and the rocks, "Fall on us and hide us from the face of him who sits on the throne and from the wrath of the Lamb! For the great day of their wrath has come, and who can stand?" (Rev. 6:15-17).

Jesus and Daniel 7's "Son of Man"

Jesus referred to His return in terms borrowed from the judgment vision of Daniel 7. He described Himself as the " 'Son of Man' " who came from heaven (see John 3:13, 31, 32; 6:50, 51, 62) and who will return " 'on the clouds of heaven,' " meaning on clouds of angels (see Dan. 7:13, 9, 10). Jesus added that He would come as the Son of Man " 'with power and great glory' " (Matt. 24:30), referring to His celestial glory spoken of in Daniel 7:14, 27. He summed up all three references to Daniel 7 in His climactic announcement: " 'They will see the Son of Man coming on the clouds of the sky, with power and great glory.' "

The connection with Daniel 7 is essential for understanding the specific sign of His appearance. Jesus not only borrowed the sign of His parousia from Daniel 7:13, He applied it to His coming *to the earth* after He had come to the Father to receive the authority to rule over the earth (Dan. 7:9-14). Take a closer look at Jesus' appli-

Daniel 7:13, 14	Matthew 24:30
"In my vision at night I looked, and there before me was *one like a son of man, coming with the clouds of heaven.* He approached the Ancient of Days and was led into his presence. *He was given authority, glory and sovereign power;* all peoples, nations and men of every language worshiped him."	"At that time *the sign of the Son of Man will appear in the sky* and all the nations of the earth will mourn. *They will see the Son of Man coming on the clouds of the sky, with power and great glory.*"

cation of His coming "with the clouds":

Under oath, Jesus solemnly declared before the high priest that He was the Messiah of prophecy and would come again as the celestial "Son of Man" of Daniel 7 who was escorted by a cloud of angels to God the Father: " 'In the future you will see the Son of Man sitting at the right hand of the Mighty One and coming on the clouds of heaven' " (Matt. 26:64). Clearly, Jesus understood His mission in the light of the victorious Judgment of Daniel 7!

The Significance of the Cosmic Signs

What then is the meaning of the darkening and shaking of the sun, moon, and stars (see Matt. 24:29)? This cosmic phenomenon should not be divorced from its biblical context, as some of the historical school of interpretation have done. It should be explained from the prophetic setting in the Hebrew prophets. These prophets regularly described cosmic signs in their judgment oracles, as the margin of Matthew 24:29 indicates. The prophets used a sudden darkening of the sun, moon, and stars as their standard image to introduce the Creator's retributive judgment on all nations that were bent on the destruction of His covenant people (see Isa. 13:10 for Babylon; Isa. 34:4 for Edom; Ezek. 32:7, 8 for Egypt; Amos 8:9; 9:5 for an apostate Israel; Joel 2:10, 31; 3:15 for an apostate Judah; Isa. 24:19, 23; Hag. 2:6, 7, 21, 22 for the hostile world).

These Old Testament passages reveal that the prophets expected more than merely astronomical signs. The cosmic events they anticipated would introduce and accompany the awesome appearance of Yahweh as the Creator and Judge of all men. Jesus adopted this theology of Israel's prophets and transformed it into a *Christ-centered* theology of cosmic signs. The high point of His prophetic discourse is the new *christological* interpretation of the Day of Yahweh (see Matt. 24:29, 30). Jesus creatively restructured the standard cosmic imagery of the prophets around His own future appearance. He taught that all the judgment oracles concerning Israel and the other nations will meet and end in Him. Consequently, the Day of God becomes the Day of the Lord Jesus. This was the news that shocked

Judaism. This fundamental truth became an essential part of the apostolic gospel (see 1 Cor. 1:8; 2 Cor. 1:14; 2 Thess. 2:2; Phil. 1:10).

A close look at the Old Testament prophecies further reveals that they were not meant to predict a specific timetable or chronological order of cosmic signs. They offer no uniform order of the cosmic imagery (see Isa. 13:10, 13; 24:18-23; 34:4, 8; Joel 2:10, 11, 28, 30, 31; 3:14-16). The Old Testament throws a fresh light on the Christ-centered application of the cosmic imagery in Matthew 24:29, 30. The ancient prophets made the cosmic upheavals an integral part of the Day of Yahweh or Judgment Day, thereby indicating that Israel's God was the Creator of heaven and earth. They did not make a chronological distinction between the "darkening" and the "shaking" of the heavenly bodies. They portrayed all these upheavals in the sky as occurring simultaneously when the Creator comes as the Judge of the world.

Jesus placed the totality of the cosmic events within the day of *His* coming to judge the world. A careful analysis of Matthew 24:27-31 by an Adventist Bible scholar led to this conclusion:

> Matthew's main concern is not to explain the identity of the signs or to provide a timetable, but to paint the coming of the Son of Man in bright colors and to move his audience into the glory of the Parousia. Determining the timetable is not Matthew's intention.[8]

Just as Luke gave a historical application of the sign of the imminent fall of Jerusalem (Luke 21:20-24), so he also gave a historical application of the cosmic signs that introduce the Second Coming (Luke 21:25-28). Luke warned against a premature expectation of immediacy (21:8), but he accepted one particular sign as valid: *the shaking of the heavenly bodies* (21:26-28). Only " 'at that time [will] they . . . see the Son of Man coming in a cloud with power and great glory' " (21:27). Luke didn't point to a timetable of intermittent cosmic signs spread through hundreds of years but to one singular cosmic shaking of "the heavenly bodies." That is the sign of the nearness of Christ's coming. " 'When these things [the shaking of the heavenly bodies] begin to take place, stand up and lift up your heads, because your redemption is drawing near' " (21:28). [For a study of the cosmic signs in Revelation, see Appendix A.]

The Grand Finale of Redemption

Jesus concluded His prophetic speech with God's promise of the gathering of the chosen people:

"He will send his angels with a loud trumpet call, and they will gather his elect from the four winds, from one end of the heavens to the other" (Matt. 24:31).

Jesus added to the visible sign an audible sign. The margin of this text rightfully points to Isaiah 27:13 and Zechariah 9:14 as the Hebrew sources of Jesus' promise. Isaiah predicted not only that Yahweh would judge Israel's enemies but also that He would gather up the scattered Israelites "one by one" and restore them in the true worship of God. "In that day a great trumpet will sound" for that very purpose (27:12, 13). Zechariah even promised that "the Sovereign LORD will sound the trumpet" in His holy war to deliver His covenant people (9:14). In other words, then, Jesus claimed that all the promises of Israel's final gathering will be fulfilled when *He* comes as the holy Warrior with His own angels and His own trumpet blast! (Obviously, Matthew 24 does not teach a secret or invisible rapture of the chosen ones.)

From the very beginning of the Jewish nation, from the days of Moses, the gathering of the Israelites from all the nations of the earth was an essential part of Israel's hope (see Deut. 30:1-4; Isa. 11:10-12; 43:5-7; 56:8; Ezek. 36:24). Jesus confirmed that He will fulfill these covenant promises of Yahweh by gathering all *His* elect to Himself (Matt. 24:31). He will not gather the twelve literal tribes of Israel to Palestine. Instead, He will gather all who by faith have accepted His Messiahship and Lordship as proclaimed in the gospel of the kingdom of God. This means that Jesus will fulfill the ancient promises for His followers among all nations, among Jews and Gentiles. Such is Jesus' new, *christocentric* perspective.

The apocalyptic consummation will be infinitely more glorious than the prophets had imagined. Myriads of angels had formed "the clouds of heaven" when they escorted the celestial "son of man" to God the Father in the last judgment (Dan. 7:9, 10, 13). Jesus calls them " '*his* angels' " (Matt. 24:31; see also 13:41; 25:31). Through these angels' work of gathering His elect from the entire earth, Jesus will realize the grand finale of redemption for all the saints in the everlasting kingdom of God and thus fulfill Daniel 7:27 and 12:2. In Matthew 24 Jesus presented the gospel's new hope, based on His atoning death and resurrection from the dead.

> "Learn this lesson from the fig tree: As soon as its twigs get tender and its leaves come out, you know that summer is near. Even so, *when you see all these things, you know that it is near, right at the door.* I tell you the truth, *this generation will certainly not pass away until all these things have happened*" (Matt. 24:32-34).

Jesus added this parable to His prophetic discourse to encourage His followers to be alert and to keep looking forward to the final redemption with absolute confidence. They should not be speculating about His soon coming when only *some* of the predicted events were fulfilled. They must expect His immediate coming only when " 'all these things' " were visibly fulfilled. In other words, we must see the fulfillment of all the signs before we can know with certainty that Jesus' coming is " 'near, right at the door.' " This emphasis on the fulfillment of " 'all these things' " is our protection against premature announcements. Only the last generation will " 'see all these things' " fulfilled, including Jesus' prediction that " 'the heavenly bodies will be shaken' " (Matt. 24:29). The generation that experiences these cosmic signs " 'will . . . not pass away until all these things have happened.' " (Verse 34. For an in-depth study of Matthew 24:34, see Appendix B).

In other words, people will see the Son of Man coming " 'on the clouds of the sky, with power and great glory' " (v. 30) *during* the "shaking" of the solar system. The time of preparation for that awesome event is now, not when the cosmic signs are taking place! " 'Therefore keep watch, because you do not know on what day your Lord will come' " (Matt. 24:42).

1. A. A. Hoekema, *The Bible and the Future* (Grand Rapids: Eerdmans, 1979), 148.
2. Samuele Bacchiocchi, *The Advent Hope for Human Hopelessness* (Berrien Springs, Mich.: Biblical Perspectives, 1986), 117.
3. G. R. Knight, *Matthew,* The Abundant Life Bible Amplifier (Nampa, Idaho: Pacific Press®, 1994), 237.
4. Book II, chapter 19; and book VI.
5. *Ecclesiastical History*, III, 5, 3.
6. Josephus, *Wars*, book VI, 5, 2.
7. So also Pheme Perkins, in *The New Interpreter's Bible* (Nashville: Abingdon Press, 1995), 8:690.
8. K. K. Kim, *The Signs of the Parousia*, Doctoral Dissertation Series, vol. 3 (Seoul, Korea: Korean Samyook University, 1994), 390.

Chapter Two

PAUL'S PREVIEW
OF
CHURCH HISTORY

Just as Jesus responded to a question from His disciples about the sign of His parousia (in Matt. 24), so Paul reacted to a misconception about the time of the Parousia held by the church in Thessalonica (2 Thess. 2). Paul's outline of future events resembles that of Jesus in Matthew 24. Paul uses the same expressions Jesus did, such as "parousia," "the clouds," His coming "like a thief in the night," and others. This fact has led some to conclude that "the words of Jesus as recorded by Matthew were the source of Paul's teaching."[1]

Paul had planted the church in Thessalonica during his second missionary journey (Acts 17:1-4). Shortly thereafter, in A.D. 50, Paul wrote two letters to that church. In his first letter he comforted grieving believers who had begun to wonder whether those among them who had died would miss the glory of the Lord's return. Paul assured them that Jesus' resurrection gives believers hope for the resurrection of their dead loved ones, "for since we believe that Jesus died and rose again, even so, through Jesus, God will bring with him those who have died" (1 Thess. 4:14, NRSV).

Paul then appealed to "the Lord's own word" (4:15), to explain in further detail that all believers will be united and meet the Lord in the air together. A comparison with Jesus' teaching shows how Paul depended on Jesus' words:

Jesus: Matthew 24:30, 31	Paul: 1 Thess. 4:16, 17
"They will see the Son of Man coming on the clouds of the sky, with power and great glory. And he will send his angels with a loud trumpet call, and they will gather his elect from the four winds, from one end of the heavens to the other."	For the Lord himself will come down from heaven, with a loud command, with the voice of the archangel and with the trumpet call of God, and the dead in Christ will rise first. After that, we who are still alive and are left will be caught up together with them in the clouds to meet the Lord in the air. And so we will be with the Lord forever.

Paul's words of comfort are strikingly similar to Jesus' words. Three concepts run parallel: (1) Jesus' descent from heaven in "the clouds," (2) the "trumpet call" of God, and (3) the worldwide gathering of the elect to Jesus. These three themes indicate that Paul knew Jesus' teachings; he simply enlarged them to comfort the grieving believers. Interestingly, the essence of this prophetic hope is found in the book of Daniel (in 7:13, 14, 27, and 12:1, 2 in particular). So we see that Jesus and Paul believed in the apocalyptic hope Daniel presented! They applied Daniel's prophecies to their own times and to the future: Jesus in Matthew 24, and Paul in 2 Thessalonians 2.

The Occasion for Second Thessalonians

Why was the apostle compelled to write a second letter to the church in Thessalonica that same year? It seems that some of the Thessalonian brethren misinterpreted his first letter. They believed it said or implied that Paul would still be alive when Jesus returned, that the end-time was therefore already present, and that Jesus' parousia could come at any time, "like a thief in the night" (1 Thess. 5:2; compare Matt. 24:43). This was, in their view, confirmed by the severe persecution they were enduring (1 Thess. 3:4). The result of this expectation of immediacy was that some stopped working for their daily bread and became disorderly and idle (see 2 Thess. 3:6-13).

Paul reacted to this serious misunderstanding of his first letter with a compelling argument derived from the book of Daniel. He began by stating that certain events must take place *before* the Parousia:

> Concerning the coming [parousia] of our Lord Jesus Christ and our being gathered to him, we ask you, brothers, not to become easily unsettled or alarmed by some prophecy, report or letter supposed to have come from us, saying that the day of the Lord has already come. Don't let anyone deceive you in any way, for that day will not come until the rebellion occurs and the man of lawlessness is revealed, the man doomed to destruction (2 Thess. 2:1-3).

Here Paul categorically rejects the idea that "the day of the Lord has already come" or that the Parousia could occur at any moment. He thus denies having taught them an immediate deliverance in his first letter. They needed more instruction about the sequence of events leading up to the day of the Lord; "they needed to have them set in their chronological relationship."[2] This is the purpose of Paul's second letter to the Thessalonians. His teaching will provide us with a guideline for interpreting the book of Revelation and its symbolic images.

Paul's Application of Daniel's Prophecy

Paul warned of a particular event that would precede Jesus' second advent—namely, the coming or parousia of the antichrist, whom Paul calls "the lawless one," or literally: "the man of lawlessness [Greek: *anomia*]." (Significantly, Jesus also predicted the increase of *anomia* in His prophetic speech in Matthew 24:12). Paul clarified the time and nature of this coming lawlessness. He called it "the apostasy" [Greek: *hê apostasia*], which means the "falling away" (KJV) from the word of God and the testimony of Jesus—about which, he reminded the Thessalonians, he had already warned them (see 2 Thess. 2:5). Paul himself had been accused of teaching "apostasy from Moses" (Acts 21:21), that is, that people should forsake the law of Moses. Apostasy from the Christian faith, however, means forsaking the law of God and the gospel of Jesus! This apostasy would be so serious that it equaled "rebellion" against God. (The risen Lord gave John the Revelator special visions that further clarified this subversion of Christianity [see Revelation 14-19, where it is called "Babylon"].)

Paul explained that the coming apostate will, like the Lord Jesus, have his "revelation" (2 Thess. 2:6, 7). Bruce aptly comments: "This suggests that he is in some sense a rival Messiah, the *antichrist* of 1 John 2:18."[3] In this respect, it is meaningful that Paul also called this man of lawlessness "the son of perdition" (2 Thess. 2:3, KJV), "the one destined for destruction" (NRSV). Jesus had used the same phrase—"the son of perdition"—to characterize Judas Iscariot (John 17:12, KJV). Judas was a leading apostle among the twelve ordained followers of Jesus. His hypocritical betrayal of Jesus belongs to the essence of apostasy!

Paul based his prediction of "the rebellion" or "the apostasy" on Daniel's prophecies. (The margins of most Bible versions provide the specific cross references from 2 Thessalonians 2:3, 4 to the Old Testament so everyone can quickly find Paul's sources.) The apostle drew specifically on Daniel's portrayals of the little horn who had "a mouth that spoke boastfully" (Dan. 7:8), of the king of chapter 8 who "will cause deceit to prosper, and . . . will consider himself superior" (v. 25), and of the king of chapter 11 who "will do as he pleases. He will exalt and magnify himself above every god and will say unheard-of things against the God of gods" (v. 36).

Paul characterized the coming "man of lawlessness [*tês*

anomias]" in these brief words:

"He will oppose and will exalt himself over everything that is called God or is worshiped, so that he sets himself up in God's temple, proclaiming himself to be God" (2 Thess. 2:4).

Paul pictured the "man of lawlessness," or antichrist, as enthroning himself in God's temple. He borrowed his language from Daniel 11:36, 37, which predicted that the self-willed king "will show no regard for the gods of his fathers or . . . any god, but will exalt himself above them all" (v. 37). He will have the same spirit as the king of Babylon whom Isaiah portrayed as aspiring to "ascend to heaven" and to make himself "like the Most High" (Isa. 14:13, 14), the same spirit as the self-deifying monarch of Tyre (Ezek. 28:2).

Daniel also revealed that this king would enter the temple of Israel's God and replace the true worship cultus with his own: "His armed forces will rise up to desecrate the temple fortress and will abolish the daily sacrifice. Then they will set up the abomination that causes desolation" (Dan. 11:31; also 8:11, 12; 12:11). Daniel predicted that this anti-God power would "take his stand *against the Prince of princes*. Yet he will be destroyed" (8:25, emphasis added). This describes the opponent of God as the anti-Messiah or antichrist, who will establish an apostate worship of himself, yet will be destroyed by the true Messiah when the latter appears in His heavenly glory.

Paul Used Daniel's Time Frame

Daniel placed this antichrist in his unique chronological framework of successive world powers. In 2 Thessalonians, Paul made Daniel's prophecy the principal source of his argument for the "timing" of the Day of the Lord. Earlier, Paul had made an explanation of Daniel's order of events a part of his teaching: "Don't you remember that when I was with you I used to tell you these things? And now you know what is holding him back, *so that he may be revealed at the proper time*" (2 Thess. 2:5) Paul didn't need to give all the details again. He simply reminded the confused believers of the basic sequence of coming events that he had taught them on the basis of Daniel: First, the antichrist and his self-worship, deceitful signs, and wonders must be revealed (2:9). Only then will Jesus' parousia take place. Paul explained, "the lawless one will be revealed," then "the Lord Jesus will overthrow [him] with the breath of his mouth and destroy [him] by the splendor of his coming" (2:8).

Just as the anti-Messiah in Daniel 8 is suddenly "destroyed, but not by human power" (v. 25) and as the king of the North will suddenly "come to his end, and no one will help him" (Dan. 11:45), so, Paul explained, the antichrist will be destroyed by the awesome appearance of Jesus, "by the splendor of his [*parousia*]" (2 Thess. 2:8). Paul applied here the very words of Isaiah, who predicted that the Messiah will come to "strike the earth with the rod of his mouth; with the breath of his lips he will slay the wicked" (Isa. 11:4).

What mattered especially to Paul was the fact that the antichrist had *not yet* set himself up as the false messiah and judge "in God's temple" (2 Thess. 2:4). Therefore, the day of the Lord could not be present and the Parousia was not imminent. He stressed this point: "Let no one deceive you in any way; for *that day will not come unless the rebellion comes first* [Greek: *prôton,* omitted in NIV] *and the lawless one is revealed*" (2:3, NRSV). Paul built his pastoral argument on the chronological order of events laid out in Daniel 7. There the prophet indicated that the anti-Messiah would arise *after* the Roman Empire had been divided into ten smaller kingdoms (Dan. 7:24).

In his night vision, Daniel had seen four imaginary beasts, representing the four successive world empires that began with Babylon and ended with the Roman Empire, which would destroy the second temple (Dan. 7:17; 9:26). This was the standard Jewish interpretation during Paul's time.[4] Jesus saw the Roman armies as the fulfillment of Daniel's prediction of the destruction of Jerusalem (Matt. 24:15-20; Luke 21:20-22). The fall of the Roman Empire was a gradual process that lasted more than a hundred years and was completed in A.D. 476. The restraining power of ancient Rome, then, was removed in the fifth century, so that the antichrist could develop freely in Europe during the Middle Ages. The implication is that the same place and throne occupied by the restrainer will be occupied subsequently by the antichrist, who functions as the successor of the Roman emperors. F. F. Bruce states: "No more convincing account of the restrainer has been suggested than that put forward by Tertullian (*De resurr. carn.* 24): 'What is this but the Roman state, whose removal when it has been divided among ten kings will bring on Antichrist?' "[5] The church fathers understood that the antichrist could not be fully revealed so long as pagan Rome remained in power.

The Christian Temple of God

It is critically important to establish the meaning of Paul's words that the antichrist will set himself up "in God's temple," or literally: "that he takes his seat in the temple of God [*eis ton naon tou theou kathisai]*, declaring himself to be God" (2 Thess. 2:4, NRSV). Paul did not think of the antichrist as an atheistic power, but as a staunchly religious one who would claim to speak instead of and on behalf of Jesus. He described the antichrist as a rival Messiah who has his own solemn parousia as a parody of Jesus' coming (v. 9).

The false messiah will also imitate the signs and wonders that Jesus performed. Paul explained:

"The coming of the lawless one will be in accordance with the work of Satan displayed in all kinds of counterfeit miracles, signs and wonders" (2 Thess. 2:9).

This threefold deceiving power parodies Jesus' ministry, which God accredited "by miracles, wonders and signs" (Acts 2:22). Jesus had warned that false messiahs and false prophets would appear "and perform great signs and miracles to deceive even the elect—if that were possible" (Matt. 24:24). Jesus' warning suggests that Satan himself will energize and authorize the antichrist by supernatural signs. Paul also mentioned this persistent satanic activity: "For the secret power of lawlessness is already at work" (2 Thess. 2:7). He thus revealed that an evil force was operating secretly behind human activity, determined to rule over God's church.

Paul used the word "temple" [*naos*] in his other letters too, but never in reference to the literal building in Jerusalem. He always meant either the church as a spiritual temple in which God's Spirit dwells or the individual soul-temple of the believer, as the following passages make clear:

What agreement is there between the temple of God and idols? For we are the temple of the living God. As God has said: "I will live with them and walk among them, and I will be their God, and they will be my people" (2 Cor. 6:16).

Don't you know that you yourselves are God's temple and that God's Spirit lives in you? (1 Cor. 3:16).

Do you not know that your body is a temple of the Holy Spirit, who is in you, whom you have received from God? (1 Cor. 6:19).

In him [Jesus] the whole building [the church] is joined together and rises to become a holy temple in the Lord (Eph. 2:21).

Paul viewed the church as a child of the "Jerusalem that is above," "she is our mother" (Gal. 4:26). When he used the phrase "the temple of God," it is clear that he meant the spiritual temple of the church, not the earthly temple in Jerusalem. That was also the understanding of the Protestant Reformation. The *Apology of the Augsburg Confession,* written by Melanchthon in 1531 and adopted as an official confession of faith by the Evangelical Lutheran Church, states: "Paul also predicts that Antichrist will 'take his seat in the temple of God' (2 Thess. 2:4); that is, that he will rule and hold office in the church."[6]

Melanchthon offered this challenging explanation in his *Treatise on the Power and Primacy of the Pope* of 1537:

The doctrine of the pope conflicts in many ways with the Gospel, and the pope arrogates to himself a threefold divine authority. First, because *he assumes for himself the right to change the doctrine of Christ and the worship instituted by God, and he wishes to have his own doctrine and worship observed as divine.* Second, because he assumes for himself . . . the jurisdiction over souls after this life. Third, because the pope is unwilling to be judged by the church or by anybody, and he exalts his authority above the decisions of councils and the whole church. *Such unwillingness to be judged by the church or by anybody is to make himself out to be God.* Finally, he defends such horrible errors and such impiety with the greatest cruelty *and puts to death those who dissent.*[7]

Interestingly, a leading Catholic exegete acknowledges that Paul unmistakably meant the Christian church when he used the phrase the "temple of God" in 2 Thessalonians 2. Charles H. Giblin comments on this text: "An ecclesial [church] interpretation is supported by the wider context of Paul's use of cult-imagery."[8] Giblin, however, interprets Paul's letter as a warning only of what *might* happen, not of what *will* happen.

The Subversion of the Gospel
The essence of the "rebellion" within Jesus' church becomes evident when we consider its claim to have His authority to forgive sins! The Jewish leaders balked at Jesus' declaration to a paralytic, " 'Friend, your sins are forgiven' " (Luke 5:20). They objected: " 'Who is this fellow who speaks blasphemy? Who can forgive sins but God alone?' " (5:21). If Jesus had not been the Son of God, the Jews would have been justified in their condemnation of Him; they had the correct definition of blasphemy (see Ps. 32:5; 1 John 1:9). For the church or anyone in it to claim what is Jesus' prerogative is an arrogant usurpation of His unique priesthood. Paul explained: "For there is one God and one mediator between God and men, the man Christ Jesus, who gave himself as a ransom for all men" (1 Tim. 2:5, 6). Salvation by a new priesthood subverts the apostolic gospel and comes under Paul's "anathema" (Gal. 1:8, 9).

Another example of the usurpation of a divine right involves the Decalogue, God's moral law, which He wrote with His own finger on tablets of stone (see Exod. 32:16). Daniel predicted that the arrogant king would try to change God's holy law:

"He shall speak words against the Most High, shall wear out the holy ones of the Most High, *and shall attempt to change the sacred seasons and the law"* (Dan. 7:25, NRSV).

Modern exegetes hold the view that Daniel 7:25 refers to the Syrian invader Antiochus IV, who did away with the Sabbath and other religious festivals of the Mosaic law during his persecution of the Jews between 167 and 164 B.C. (1 Macc. 1:41-64). But this brief episode under the old covenant was only a partial fulfillment or anticipation of Daniel's prophecy. That Daniel was announcing a persecution of the saints under the new covenant is clear because he pictured the "little horn" arising *after* the Roman Empire had been partitioned (Dan. 7:23, 24). The papacy is responsible for the integration of the pagan Sunday law into her ecclesiastical law. Church history reveals that the Roman Church demanded Sunday observance and forbade Sabbath keeping. In the year 538, the Third Synod of Orleans even decreed punishment for those who would not come to church to worship on Sunday.[9]

Paul concluded his instruction about the future by announcing that God will test His people to see whether or not they have a love for the truth (2 Thess. 2:11, 12).

Parallels Between 2 Thessalonians 2 and Matthew 24

Paul's teaching in 2 Thessalonians 2 runs parallel to that of Jesus in Matthew 24; note the italicized words below:

Jesus: Matthew 24	Paul: 2 Thessalonians 2
"Watch out that no one deceives you. For many will come in my name, claiming, 'I am the Christ,' and will deceive many" (vv. 4, 5).	*Don't let anyone deceive you in any way* (v. 3). We ask you, brothers, not to become easily unsettled . . . [as

Jesus: Matthew 24	Paul: 2 Thessalonians 2
"At that time *many will turn away from the faith* and will betray and hate each other, and *many false prophets will appear and deceive many people.* Because of the increase of wickedness [anomia], the love of most will grow cold, but he who stands firm to the end will be saved" (vv. 10-13).	if] the day of the Lord has already come (vv. 1, 2).
"So when you see standing in the holy place 'the abomination that causes desolation,' spoken of through the prophet Daniel" (v. 15).	That day will not come *until the rebellion [apostasia] occurs and the man of lawlessness [anomia] is revealed,* the man doomed for destruction (v. 3).
"For false Christs and false prophets will appear and perform great signs and miracles to deceive the elect—if that were possible" (v. 24).	And now you know what is holding him back, *so that he may be revealed at the proper time* (v. 6). The coming of the lawless one will be in accordance with the work of Satan displayed in all kinds of *counterfeit miracles, signs and wonders,* and in every sort of evil that deceives those who are perishing (vv. 9, 10).
"At that time the sign of the Son of Man will appear in the sky, and all the nations of the earth will mourn" (v. 30).	Then the lawless one will be revealed, whom the Lord Jesus will overthrow with the breath of his mouth and destroy by the splendor of his coming (v. 8).

Both Jesus and Paul began their prophetic discourses with warnings against deceivers and self-styled messiahs. Both end the church age with Jesus' glorious appearing as the Judge and Redeemer of all people. Both emphasize a delay of Jesus' return because of a horrible sacrilege that will arise in the "holy place" or "God's temple" (Matt. 24:15; 2 Thess. 2:4). Both Jesus and Paul attempted to cool down an apocalyptic fever that expected Jesus' parousia prematurely.

Paul's particular concern with the *timing* of the antichrist led him to stress that the "lawless one" will be revealed publicly *"at the proper time"* (2 Thess. 2:6, emphasis added). To interpret

2 Thessalonians 2 correctly, his outline of church history must be placed against the background of Daniel's chronological sequence.

Clearly, to see the full biblical picture of the church age, we must study the prophecies of Daniel, Jesus, Paul, and John's Apocalypse together. They illuminate each other because they describe the same epoch of salvation history that ends in Jesus' coming with the glory of God and His angels.

All biblical witnesses agree that religious apostasy will intensify in the time of the end. Revelation 13–19 portrays this final development and the proliferation of supernatural signs and deceiving miracles that accompanies it. Revelation emphasizes that "deception" will occur through miraculous signs by demonic spirits in the end time (Rev. 13:13, 14; 16:13, 14; 19:20). Paul warned believers to be on the alert for teachers who claim to be Jesus' apostles yet teach a false gospel and way of salvation:

> Such men are false apostles, deceitful workmen, masquerading as apostles of Christ. And no wonder, for Satan himself masquerades as an angel of light. It is not surprising, then, if his servants masquerade as servants of righteousness. Their end will be what their actions deserve (2 Cor. 11:13-15).

Those who rely on signs and miracles ignore the inspired standard by which we are to judge all supernatural signs. Moses warned Israel not to follow a prophet who performed "a miraculous sign or wonder" and then "preached rebellion against the LORD your God," saying, " 'Let us follow other gods . . . and let us worship them' " (Deut. 13:1-6). Such a "detestable thing" in Israel was to be "investigated thoroughly" (v. 14) and such "wicked men" (v. 13) were to be put to death (v. 9). We must never consider miracles the ultimate norm of truth. Scripture says: "To the law and to the testimony! If they do not speak according to this word, they have no light of dawn" (Isa. 8:20). John advanced this criterion for Christians as "the word of God and the testimony of Jesus" (Rev. 1:2, 9; 20:4) as determined by the Old and New Testaments.

Jesus Himself overcame Satan's enticements by clinging to the written Word of God. Three times He repeated "it is written" to repel the efforts of the evil one to lead Him to worship a creature instead of God (see Matt. 4:1-10). This is how Jesus remained faithful. So it's no surprise, then, that Paul urged the believers of Thessalonica to "stand firm and hold to the teachings we passed on to you, whether by word of mouth or by letter" (2 Thess. 2:15). Similarly, several times the book of Revelation mentions that the saints overcame Satan "by the blood of the Lamb and by the word of their testimony" (12:11; cf. 1:9; 6:9; 12:17; 20:4). Jesus promised, "He who stands firm to the end will be saved" (Matt. 24:13).

It is not sufficient to know the antichrist of the past. We need to arm ourselves with a correct understanding of the prophetic word of God for our time and for the end of the age. Enlightened by this knowledge, we will no longer be ignorant of Satan's schemes (2 Cor. 2:11).

---

1. G. H. Waterman, "The Sources of Paul's Teaching on the Second Coming in 1 and 2 Thessalonians," *Journal of the Evangelical Theological Society*, 18/2 (1975):105-113.
2. F. F. Bruce, *1 & 2 Thessalonians*, Word Biblical Commentary (Waco, Tex.: Word Books, 1982), 45:166.
3. Ibid., 167.
4. See LeRoy E. Froom, *The Prophetic Faith of Our Fathers* (Hagerstown, Md.: Review and Herald, 1950), 1:197-204.
5. Bruce, 171.
6. Articles 7, 8, "The Church," *The Book of Concord*, Th. G. Tappert, ed. (Philadelphia: Fortress Press, 1959), 169.
7. "The Marks of the Antichrist," ibid., 327; emphasis added.
8. *The Threat to Faith: An Exegetical and Theological Re-examination of 2 Thessalonians*, AnBib., (Rome: Pontifical Biblical Institute, 1967), 31:78.
9. Canon 28; see C. J. Hefele, *A History of the Councils of the Church* (Edinburgh: Clark, 1895), 4:209.

Chapter Three

ASSURANCES
FROM THE
SEALED SCROLL

The book of Revelation serves a unique purpose in the New Testament. It sums up the Hebrew Bible and adds the gospel's fresh assurance that Jesus Christ will fulfill Israel's hope. No other Bible book stresses so strongly the essential unity of the Hebrew and Christian faiths. In Revelation we find a new blend, one that combines Israel's language and images with the portrayals that John described as "the revelation [or "apocalypse"] of Jesus Christ, which God gave him to show his servants what must soon take place" (Rev. 1:1).

The Apocalypse claims that the God of Israel has spoken in Jesus of Nazareth as the risen Lord and Revelator. Here Jesus speaks with messianic authority to His church universal, to alert her to what will threaten her faith until He returns to complete the redemption of the world. More than that, He reassures His followers that His death as the Lamb of God was not in vain; it is the very foundation of His authority to rule in righteousness and peace over His church and all humankind. The book of Revelation presents Jesus as both the conquering Messiah and the atoning Passover Lamb.

The title "the Lamb (of God)" occurs twenty-eight times in the Apocalypse. It expresses the connection between Jesus' earthly mission and His present ministry as heavenly King-Priest. John's sublime vision of the entire universe's worship of the Creator introduces the celestial Jesus as "the Lamb" (Rev. 4, 5). John witnessed here what has often been called Jesus' "enthronement" as the heavenly King. Actually, this scene may be described more accurately as the "investiture" of the Lamb. This grand vision is not merely a peripheral scene; it stands as the divine legitimation of Jesus' imperial power, honor, glory, and praise as portrayed through the rest of the Apocalypse.

This "Lamb of God," the risen Jesus, summoned John to see "what must take place after this" (Rev. 4:1) and bestowed on him the Spirit of prophecy (see v. 2). Then John viewed the awesome throne of God and heard the cosmic adoration of God in His worthiness as Creator of all things (4:2-11).

Worthy to Open the Scroll

John wrote:

> I saw in the right hand of him who sat on the throne a scroll with writing on both sides and sealed with seven seals. And I saw a mighty angel proclaiming in a loud voice, "Who is worthy to break the seals and open the scroll?" (Rev. 5:1, 2).

The heavenly scroll [Greek: *biblion*] takes the center of attention in this vision. At first, to John's distress, no one is found who can open it or look inside it; no one is "worthy" to do so (Rev. 5:2-4). Then an elder* announces that there is One who can open the scroll and its seals because of the moral victory His life and death won:

> "The Lion of the tribe of Judah, the Root of David, has triumphed. He is able to open the scroll and its seven seals."

---

*The elders may represent the unfallen worlds.

Then *I saw a Lamb, looking as if it had been slain, standing in the center of the throne,* encircled by the four living creatures and the elders (Rev. 5:5, 6).

Remarkably, the risen Lord is not given this honor because He has become King but because He has "triumphed" (v. 5) and proved to be "worthy" (v. 4). The elders and the living creatures fall down before the Lamb and begin to sing this "new song" (v. 9):

"You are worthy to take the scroll and to open its seals, because you were slain, and with your blood you purchased men for God from every tribe and language and people and nation. You have made them to be a kingdom and priests to serve our God, and they will reign on the earth" (Rev. 5:9, 10).

This song declares that the risen Jesus is worthy to execute God's plan to save the lost planet because He has ransomed all people by His infinite self-sacrifice. Then myriads of angels add their sevenfold praise: "Worthy is the Lamb, who was slain . . ." (Rev. 5:12). And finally, all creatures in the cosmos raise an anthem in worship "to him who sits on the throne and to the Lamb" (5:13).

Apparently, the term "worthy" is a key word of the entire vision. Why was this "worthiness" required to open the book of divine providence that God held? Only someone who has stood God's test is "worthy" for that honor—and it was the Messiah from the house of David who stood that test by His moral victory! He did not triumph as a powerful, glorious king but as a slain lamb, though one with divine attributes. This sharpens the focus on the sacrifice of this Lamb of God, who bears the marks of His sacrifice in His glorified body and whose work of redemption stirs the singing of new songs in heaven. He has ransomed slaves from all nations and has made them, even Gentiles, to be the holy people of God, priests and kings—once the prerogative of ancient Israel alone (see Exod. 19:5, 6). So, the new song of Revelation 5:9, 10 announces that Jesus has made His followers the New Israel, honored with the same priestly mission and hope as Israel under Moses.

Because of His unique qualification as the "Lion of the tribe of Judah, the Root of David" (Rev. 5:5), Jesus is declared worthy to fulfill the covenant promises God made regarding the future of the world. The sealed scroll in God's right hand contains the destiny He's planned for the world, which Jesus has agreed to accomplish. A certain parallel can be seen in Moses' decree that a newly crowned king had to take the book of the covenant from the priests and to make a copy of it so that he would faithfully execute his reign according to God's will (Deut. 17:18-20; 2 Kings 11:12; 23:1-3). The sealed scroll of Revelation 5, however, contains God's plan for all human history, including the end-time scenario as unfolded in the rest of Revelation. With the transfer of the prophetic scroll, the fate of humankind is placed into the hands of the glorified Jesus. His possession of the scroll signifies His right to rule over all humankind because of what He has done and who He is. This vision assures Christian believers that Jesus will achieve the final victory over Satan, sin, and evil.

The Essence of the Seven Seals

Revelation 6 portrays the church's witness and the world's resistance of it, extending from the inception of the church up to Jesus' return as the Judge of all men. The seals point first to the victorious power of the gospel and then to the bitter fruits of apostasy and rebellion against the gospel message. Then they announce the messianic judgments on the persecutors and murderers of Jesus' witnesses.

I watched as the Lamb opened the first of the seven seals. Then I heard one of the four living creatures say in a voice like thunder, "Come!" I looked, and there before me was a white horse! Its rider held a bow, and he was given a crown [*stephanos*], and he rode out as a conqueror bent on conquest. When the Lamb opened the second seal . . . another horse came out, a fiery red one. Its rider was given power to take peace from the earth and to make men slay each other. To him was given a large sword. When the Lamb opened the third seal . . . there before me was a black horse! Its rider was holding a pair of scales in his hand. . . . When the Lamb opened the fourth seal . . . there before me was a pale horse! Its rider was named Death, and Hades was following close behind him. They were given power over a fourth of the earth to kill by sword, famine and plague, and by the wild beasts of the earth (Rev. 6:1-8).

The first four seals—the four symbolic horses and their riders—form a textual unit that covers the entire Christian Age. These horsemen do not replace each other but join each other, much like a quartet piece in which one singer begins and then, one by one, the other three join the first, so that finally all four sing together. A parallel can be seen in the vision of the three angels of Revelation 14:6-12. These angels begin one after the other, yet they continue together as one threefold message till the Second Advent. This view does not suggest a specific timetable for the four seals.

The woes portrayed in seals two through four—war, famine, pestilence, wild beasts (Rev. 6:8)—repeat the covenant curses of the Old Testament (see Lev. 26:21-26; Deut. 32:23-25, 41-43). Ezekiel prophesied that God would discipline Jerusalem with His "four dreadful judgments—*sword and famine and wild beasts and plague*" (14:21). These plagues were not God's final judgments. They were intended to lead His wayward people to repentance so God could restore the covenant blessings. Hosea expresses beautifully this higher purpose:

"Come, let us return to the LORD. He has torn us to pieces but he will heal us; he has injured us but he will bind up our wounds. After two days he will revive us; on the third day he will restore us, that we may live in his presence" (Hos. 6:1, 2).

That's how Jesus deals with the Christian church! When the postapostolic church began to reject the gospel message of salvation by grace through faith in Jesus as offered by the rider on the white horse (Rev. 6:1, 2), the covenant curses began to come down on an apostate people as if they were arrows unleashed by the first cavalier. In short, it can be said: "The four horses . . . outline both the trend of history at the beginning of the Christian Era, and the general realities of the Christian Age."[1]

The different colors of the symbolic horses—white, red, black, and pale—suggest their different missions in God's plan. The white horse fittingly represents the gospel's conquest, the red horse the resulting persecution, and the black and the pale horses the increasing consequences of rejection of that gospel. This implies that the preaching of the gospel does not eliminate the evil in the world; rather, it exposes it (see John 3:19, 20). In this respect, history will be repeated. The past will become the future again. While the apocalyptic riders found their initial fulfillment in the apostasy and persecutions of a compromising church in past centuries, they all continue to ride until the second coming of Jesus. In particular, the rider on the white horse will go forth triumphantly once more, as the sealing message of Revelation 7 and the threefold message of Revelation 14 indicate. In the last generation the earth will again be "illuminated" by the splendor of the gospel (see Mark 13:10; Rev. 14:6, 7; 18:1).

Many modern expositors prefer to apply the rider on the white horse of Revelation 6 to secular warfare. But that application fails to connect this horse with salvation history and with the cries of the martyrs the fifth seal contains. In Revelation the seals serve to picture both the resistance to the Christian witness and the ultimate vindication of the testimony of Jesus (Rev. 6:9-11; cf. 20:4). The fifth and sixth seals place all church history in the light of the judgment of God *and* of the Lamb (6:15-17).

Parallels in Jesus' Prophetic Speech

Many recognize that the seals reproduce the features of Jesus' prophetic speech in the Gospels. British exegete R. H. Charles concluded: "The more closely we study the Seals in connection with Mark xiii, Matt. xxiv, Luke xxi, the more strongly we shall be con-

vinced that our author [John] finds his chief and controlling authority
in the eschatological scheme there set forth."[2] Charles demonstrated
that the lists of signs of the church age in Matthew and Luke recur in
the same order in Revelation 6, as his table of comparison shows[3]:

Matthew 24	Luke 21	Revelation 6 (Seals)
1. Wars	1. Wars	1. Wars
2. International strife	2. International strife	2. International strife
3. Famines	3. Earthquakes	3. Famine
4. Earthquakes	4. Famines	4. Pestilence (death)
5. Persecutions	5. *Pestilence*	5. Persecutions
6. Eclipses of sun and moon, falling stars, shaking of the heavenly bodies	6. Persecutions	6. Great earthquake, eclipse of sun, moon turns blood-red, stars fall to earth, sky recedes like a scroll; *global fear for the Day of the Wrath of God and of the Lamb*
	7. Signs in sun, moon, stars. *Global fear because of the shaking of the heavenly bodies*	

The seals combine the signs listed by Matthew 24 and Luke 21
(note the inclusion of pestilence and the global fear of the impending judgment). They omit the local earthquakes listed in the
Gospels, describing instead in the sixth seal a worldwide quake.
Revelation's disasters grow in intensity and scope, from social and
regional upheavals in seals one through four to the cosmic-universal
judgments of God in the fifth and sixth seals. In short, the progression of Revelation 6 emphasizes the sovereign rulership of God and
the Lamb over the world and assures Jesus' followers that faithfulness to "the word of God and to the testimony of Jesus" will be gra-
ciously rewarded.

The fifth seal comforts the countless gospel witnesses whose
lives were sacrificed because of the miscarriages of justice in human

courts but who trusted the faithful covenant God (see Rev. 6:9-11). The horrible persecution of Christians in Rome under Nero in John's time (A.D. 64-68) was only the beginning of the long history of cruel intolerance and injustice that continued under other Roman emperors and popes.[4] This leads to a significant conclusion: If the seals of Revelation 6 repeat and expand the signs for the church age contained in Matthew 24 and Luke 21, then, like those signs, the seals *also* span the centuries of the entire church age that ends with the return of Jesus.

The portrayals of the seals do not depend exclusively on Jesus' prophetic speech in the Gospels. They also borrow directly from the Hebrew prophets. Commentators agree that the first four seals (Rev. 6:1-8) reflect the imagery of the colored horses found in the prophet Zechariah (1:8; 6:1-8). While that ancient prophet depicted his four horses as messengers of God sent in the four directions of the earth, in Revelation these symbolic horses are transformed into agents of *messianic judgment*. The judgments of the first four seals are limited calamities (Rev. 6:8), intended to lead people to repentance. So, they have a redemptive purpose, as we've already seen regarding the rider on the white horse. Seals 2-4 show an increased hardening of the rejecters of the gospel. This process continues till it reaches its culmination in the final events, which the visions of Revelation 12–14 unfold more fully.

Divine Assurances From the Fifth Seal

When he opened the fifth seal, I saw under the altar the souls of those who had been *slain because of the word of God and the testimony they had maintained*. They called out in a loud voice, "How long, Sovereign Lord, holy and true, until you judge the inhabitants of the earth and avenge our blood?" Then each of them was given a white robe, and they were told to wait a little longer, until the number of their fellow servants and brothers who were to be killed as they had been was completed (Rev. 6:9-11).

The fifth seal is linked to the earlier seals. It focuses on the martyrs who died a violent death under the first seals, announcing a persecution still to come in the time of the end (Rev. 6:9-11). This seal describes the true witnesses and martyrs as those who were slain *"because of the word of God and the testimony they had maintained"* (6:9). This "testimony" was not merely their personal witness to Jesus, but specifically the historic testimony that Jesus Himself had given—that is, His teachings of the gospel as recorded in the New Testament (see John 3:13, 31-33). John explains that he was banished to the island of Patmos "because of the word of God and the testimony of Jesus" (Rev. 1:9). He uses this twofold phrase, with some variations, six times, presenting it as the standard of truth that distinguishes faithful worshipers from apostates *in every epoch of the church age.* (See 1:2, 9; 6:9; 12:17; 14:12; 20:4. For an extensive treatment of the biblical meaning of the phrase "the testimony of Jesus" in the book of Revelation, see Appendix C.)

The symbolic image of the martyred "souls under the altar" who cry out to God for justice should be understood in the context of Scripture and not of Greek philosophy. Notice the expression the book of Genesis uses to say that God held Cain accountable for the murder of his brother Abel: " 'What have you done? Listen! *Your brother's blood cries out to me from the ground'* " (4:10). This figure of speech means that God acknowledges that justice needs to be done for those who died a violent death because they worshiped Him. He will not forget their witness for Him! Hebrew usage indicates that their shed "blood" represents their life and soul (see Lev. 17:11, 14; Deut. 12:23; Ezek. 33:4). David affirmed, "For he who avenges blood remembers; he does not ignore the cry of the afflicted" (Ps. 9:12). And Jesus confirmed that God will remember and avenge "the righteous blood" of all the martyrs since Abel (Matt. 23:35).

Yet the martyrs were told they must "wait a little longer" before they could receive their glorious inheritance—until the final persecution is completed (Rev. 6:11). Then *all* faithful ones will enter their inheritance together, as stated in the Letter to the Hebrews: "These were all commended for their faith, yet none of them received what had been promised. God had planned something bet-

ter for us *so that only together with us would they be made perfect"*
(Heb. 11:39, 40).

In a sense, all who have died for their faith have died on "the
altar" of God (Rev. 6:9). Their blood has been poured out like sacri-
ficial blood "at the base of the altar of burnt offering" (Lev. 4:7).
Paul considered his impending martyrdom under Nero a sacrifice to
God (see 2 Tim. 4:6). Jesus assured His disciples that God would
" 'grant justice to his chosen ones who cry to him day and night' "
(Luke 18:7, NRSV). The fifth seal promises that God will not forget
any of His witnesses; He'll bring them all back to life in the resurrection of the righteous. Jesus declared to the Sadducees, "who say
there is no resurrection" (Luke 20:27),

> "in the account of the bush, even Moses showed that *the dead
> rise*, for he calls the Lord 'the God of Abraham, and the God of
> Isaac, and the God of Jacob.' *He is not the God of the dead, but
> of the living, for to him all are alive"* (Luke 20:37, 38).

The book of Daniel also offers clear assurance: "Multitudes who
sleep in the dust of the earth will awake: some to everlasting life,
others to shame and everlasting contempt" (Dan. 12:2).

What wonderful security these promises offer the believers in the
God of Israel! Hope of the resurrection is firmly rooted in the
covenant promises.

The fifth seal contains another comforting declaration: "Each of
them was given a white robe" (Rev. 6:11). This announcement
means that each persevering believer receives divine vindication.
Each of them is judged as being an overcomer and worthy of the
"white robe." This symbol was also part of the promise to the
church in Sardis: "He who overcomes will, like them, be dressed in
white. I will never blot out his name from the book of life, but will
acknowledge his name before my Father and his angels" (3:5). The
point here is that the risen Christ gives overcomers the "white
robe," which represents His own righteousness that covers our guilt
and shame (see 3:18). The following explanation by the angel
depicts this graphically: "These are they who have come out of the

great tribulation; they have washed their robes and made them white in the blood of the Lamb" (7:14).

The metaphor of washing one's robe in the blood of the Lamb stands for our daily exercise of faith in Jesus as our Substitute and Surety before God. The "white robe" stands for the gift of divine justification in the last judgment, which the believer may claim even now (see Rev. 3:18; Rom. 8:1, 33, 34). The "blood of the Lamb" is humanity's only redemption from "the wrath of the Lamb" under the sixth seal (Rev. 6:16, 17). And only "those who wash [present tense!] their robes" have "the right to the tree of life and may go through the gates into the city [the New Jerusalem]" (22:14).

The Eager Waiting of All Creation

Paul wrote: "The creation waits in eager expectation for the sons of God to be revealed. . . . Not only so, but we ourselves, who have the firstfruits of the Spirit, groan inwardly as we wait eagerly for our adoption as sons, *the redemption of our bodies*. For in this hope we were saved" (Rom. 8:19, 23, 24). The Christian hope is not based on belief in the natural immortality of the soul, which the pagan Greek philosophers Socrates and Plato taught. Instead, it is based on faith in the resurrection of the body. Paul does not expect a deliverance *from* the body but a deliverance *of* the body itself! This is the biblical hope, rooted in the power of the Creator-Redeemer.

The Christian martyrs John's Apocalypse pictures also hold firmly to this belief. They do not mistrust the sovereignty of the Lord of history. On the contrary, they stand on God's promises and look eagerly for their fulfillment. The shed blood of the martyrs cries " 'How long, Sovereign Lord, holy and true, until you judge the inhabitants of the earth and avenge our blood?' " (Rev. 6:10). This fervent hope corresponds with that highlighted in the book of Daniel: " 'How long will it take for the vision . . . of the host that will be trampled underfoot?' " (Dan. 8:13). There the angel explained that a specific end-time distress must occur before the resurrection takes place (Dan. 12:1, 2).

The thematic correspondence between the fifth seal and Daniel's visions throws light on this seal. We see that its purview includes the entire church age and the time of the end, reaching to the judgment scene of the sixth seal. The heavenly vindication of the maligned saints will be consummated by God's executive judgments on the wicked and the righteous as depicted in the sixth seal. So, the fifth and sixth seals form an indissoluble unit. Note the striking correspondence between the cry for divine vindication and vengeance in the fifth seal, on the one hand, and its historical fulfillment after the final plagues: "He *has condemned* the great prostitute who corrupted the earth by her adulteries. He *has avenged* on her the blood of his servants" (Rev. 19:2).

The Sixth Seal: Summary of Israel's Apocalyptic Outlook

I watched as he opened the sixth seal. There was a great earthquake. The sun turned black like sackcloth made of goat hair, the whole moon turned blood red, and the stars in the sky fell to earth, as late figs drop from a fig tree when shaken by a strong wind. The sky receded like a scroll, rolling up, and every mountain and island was removed from its place. Then the kings of the earth, the princes, the generals, the rich, the mighty, and every slave and every free man hid in caves and among the rocks of the mountains. They called to the mountains and the rocks, *"Fall on us and hide us from the face of him who sits on the throne and from the wrath of the Lamb! For the great day of their wrath has come, and who can stand?"* (Rev. 6:12-17).

Israel's apocalyptic hope illumines the theological message of the sixth seal. This seal presents an ingenious blending of Hebrew prophecies that deal with the Day of Yahweh. The sixth seal transforms that Day, with its cosmic upheavals, into a Christ-centered Day of Judgment and deliverance! This is the essence of the sixth seal. John's narrative adopts the traditional language with which the prophets describe the awesome appearance of the Creator as the Judge of all men. The Old Testament theophanies (manifestations of

God) are often introduced by an earthquake, dark clouds, flashes of lightning, and thunder claps or trumpet blasts (see Exod. 19:16-19; Pss. 68:7, 8; 144:5, 6; Isa. 64:1, 3; Hab. 3:1-6). These frightening phenomena in the natural world serve the high purpose of identifying the Creator as the covenant God who manifested Himself in the same dramatic way on Mount Sinai before Israel and in His holy wars against His enemies.

In the prophets' portrayals of the final judgment, they included a global earthquake that would shake both the earth and the heavenly bodies (see Joel 2:10, 11; Isa. 2:19-21; 13:10-13; Zeph. 1:2, 3; Hag. 2:6, 7). The prophets did not intend to use figurative language here. The New Testament applies Haggai's prediction of a shaking of heaven and earth as the introduction to the messianic glory to a literal shaking of the earth at the second coming of Jesus:

> At that time [under Moses] his voice shook the earth, but now he has promised, "Once more I will shake not only the earth, but also the heavens" [Hag. 2:6]. The words "once more" indicate the removing of what can be shaken—that is, created things—so that what cannot be shaken may remain. Therefore, since we are receiving a kingdom that cannot be shaken, let us be thankful, and so worship God acceptably with reverence and awe, for our "God is a consuming fire" (Heb. 12:26-29).

The sixth seal begins with a "great earthquake" accompanied by the shaking of the heavenly bodies (Rev. 6:12-14). Then follows a description of the effect of these upheavals on the world population (6:15-17). If we compare these cosmic signs with those in Matthew 24 and Luke 21, we notice that the sixth seal expands both the number of the signs and their impact. The Gospel accounts do not mention the global earthquake or the moon turning red or the stars falling "to earth, as late figs drop from a fig tree when shaken by a strong wind." The sixth seal enlarges the "shaking" of the heavens with the shaking of the earth: "The sky receded like a scroll, rolling up, and every mountain and island was removed from its place" (Rev. 6:14). The reason for this cosmic quake is disclosed in the words: *"Earth and sky fled from his presence"* (Rev. 20:11). The seventh plague expands this theophany, indicating that the mighty voice of God Himself will cause the cosmic quake after human probation has ended (Rev. 16:17-21; cf. 15:1, 5-8).

Revelation 6:12-17 vividly portrays the worldwide impact of the cosmic signs. This scene adopts Isaiah's imagery of Israel's remorse and despair in the day of Yahweh. Here we learn that God's appearance causes the cosmic quake:

> Go into the rocks, hide in the ground from dread of the LORD and the splendor of his majesty! . . . Men will flee to caves in the rocks and to holes in the ground from dread of the LORD and the splendor of his majesty, *when he rises to shake the earth* (Isa. 2:10, 19, see also v. 21).

Hosea announced the judgment to Israel in similar words: "Then they will say to the mountains, 'Cover us!' and to the hills, 'Fall on us!' " (Hos. 10:8). In the sixth seal John applied these Hebrew oracles of the day of Yahweh to the second coming of the Lamb. In so doing, he identified the day of Yahweh with the day of Jesus' return. The end-time people on earth will hide "from the face of him who sits on the throne *and from the wrath of the Lamb! For the great day of their wrath has come,* and who can stand?" (Rev. 6:16, 17).

God's Answer to the Ultimate Question

When this day of the Lord arrives, the ultimate question of the people of the world will be: "Who can stand?" Israel's prophets had raised this very question in Old Testament times (see Joel 2:11; Nah. 1:6; Mal. 3:2). Their answer was that true repentance provided the key to standing in the day of divine wrath (Joel 2:12-27; Nah. 1:7; Mal. 3:3, 4). The prophets insisted that Yahweh provides the only "refuge in times of trouble. He cares for those who trust in him" (Nah. 1:7; cf. Joel 3:16).

How does John answer this question? A whole new vision—one that appears in one of the most comforting chapters in the book of Revelation, namely chapter 7—provides the answer. This passage furnishes special encouragement for the last generation of Jesus' followers, those whom the antichrist will press to renounce their obedience to "the word of God and the testimony of Jesus." Only the power of God at work in them will enable them to stand in the hour of trial.

John saw this portrayed by the angel, "coming up from the east, having the seal of the living God" (Rev. 7:2). This "seal" is the sign of both divine approval and protection of the last generation of saints. No harm can come to them because they've been judged in heaven and placed under the seal of protection that the angels have put "on the foreheads of the servants of our God" (7:3). John "heard the number of those who were sealed: 144,000 from all the tribes of Israel" (7:4).

This reference to spiritual "Israelites" and their being sealed on the forehead points back to Ezekiel's prophecy of the outpouring of God's wrath on a rebellious Jerusalem. Ezekiel saw God's work of bringing His retributive judgment on an impenitent Jerusalem in the days of the Babylonian king Nebuchadnezzar (see Ezek. 8). The glory of God had departed from the apostate city (Ezek. 9:3), and the agents of judgment were ready to execute a terrible slaughter in the city (9:1, 2). But before the judgment began, God sent a priestly figure ahead of the angels who would carry out the judgment. This man, who had a writing kit at his side, received the command: " 'Go throughout the city of Jerusalem and *put a mark on the foreheads of those who grieve and lament over all the detestable things that are done in it*' " (9:4). In this way God separated spiritual Israel from apostate Israel. God's justice was executed only after the angel of mercy had completed his sealing work (9:6).

Ezekiel's vision clarifies the purpose of the sealing of the last generation of God's people and of their final separation from the impenitent ones. The final seal marks those who belong to Jesus and who stand under His protection. Regarding the specific number of those sealed, Bruce M. Metzger explains: "The explicit number, 144,000, symbolizes completeness—not one of the redeemed is missing."[5] All who are sealed will survive Armageddon and enter the

New Jerusalem! And Revelation 7 ends with this generous assurance to them:

> Never again will they hunger; never again will they thirst. The sun will not beat upon them, nor any scorching heat. For the Lamb at the center of the throne will be their shepherd; he will lead them to springs of living water. And God will wipe away every tear from their eyes (Rev. 7:16, 17).

---

1. Jon Paulien, *Symposium on Revelation,* Frank B. Holbrook, ed. (Silver Spring, Maryland: Biblical Research Institute, 1992), Book I:234.
2. R. H. Charles, *The Revelation of St. John,* The International Critical Commentary (Edinburgh: T. & T. Clark, 1975) vol. 1:158.
3. Ibid., slightly adapted.
4. See, e.g., *Foxe's Book of Martyrs* (Grand Rapids, Mich.: Baker Books, 1995) and Henry Charles Lea, *The Inquisition of the Middle Ages* (Lanham, Md.: Barnes & Noble Books, 1993).
5. Bruce M. Metzger, *Breaking the Code* (Nashville: Abingdon Press, 1993), 61.

Chapter Four

THE STRUCTURE OF JOHN'S AMAZING APOCALYPSE

The last book of the Bible is called the *Revelation,* or *Apocalypse,* of John because a prophet named John wrote it near the end of the first century of the Christian era. Church tradition identifies this man with John the son of Zebedee, one of the twelve apostles. Revelation was intended to encourage the churches in the Roman province of Asia Minor (now Turkey) in the face of persecution and to warn them against the dangers of apostasy. M. C. Tenney noted that John encouraged the churches to persevere in the faith by focusing on the coming of Jesus "to judge His enemies, to deliver the church from peril, and to establish the city of God."

The very first words of the Apocalypse are significant: "The revelation of Jesus Christ, which God gave him to show his servants what must soon take place" (Rev. 1:1). These words assert that the risen Lord Jesus—and not John—is the true Author of the Apocalypse. His authorship gives the book of Revelation its supreme authority and universal value for Christians. This book contains a message from the Lord of the church—a message that helps believers to prepare for His second advent; a message that becomes increasingly important as time goes by.

Relation of Form and Content

The Apocalypse is written in a unique literary form in which Hebrew terms and images are marvelously blended with gospel promises. The book as a whole shows an ingenious architectural design, with a beautiful symmetry of composition. There is a close relation between literary style and theological content—so much so that the very structure of the book highlights certain aspects of Jesus' message for the church. Consequently, we need to pay attention to Revelation's internal arrangement.

We may compare the Apocalypse with a seven-branched lampstand, or menorah. The three branches on the left of the central stem flow gradually into the three branches on the right, as their counterparts. This pattern fits the structure of the Apocalypse, which clearly has two main divisions. Chapters 1–14 focus mainly on Jesus' care for the struggling church, while chapters 15–22 focus on Jesus' second advent and the rewards He will bring with Him. This structure suggests that the book has two concerns: Jesus' priestly ministry during the church age, and His work in the final judgment.

1. Seven Letters–Revelation 1-3
2. Seven Seals–Revelation 4-7
3. Seven Trumpets–Revelation 8-9
4. End-time Message–Revelation 10-14
5. Seven Bowls–Revelation 15-18
6. Songs of Triumph–Revelation 19-20
7. New Jerusalem–Revelation 21-22

John's vision of the risen Jesus who ministers as a priest among the seven lampstands is a representative passage from the first division of the Apocalypse:

When I saw him, I fell at his feet as though dead. Then he placed his right hand on me and said: "Do not be afraid. I am the First and the Last. I am the Living One; I was dead, and behold I am alive for ever and ever! And I hold the keys of death and Hades" (Rev. 1:17, 18).

The second division of the Apocalypse centers in another assurance from the living Jesus:

"Behold, I am coming soon! My reward is with me, and I will give to everyone according to what he has done. I am the Alpha and the Omega, the First and the Last, the Beginning and the End" (Rev. 22:12, 13).

These two passages show the twofold theme: Jesus' sustaining ministry today, and His future work of deliverance at the Second Advent. Chapters 1 to 14 deal largely with Jesus' work to keep His church alive and to make her His witness in the world. Chapters 15 to 22 focus on the last judgment and the rewards that come at Jesus' second coming.

Striking Counterparts

A close look at the structure of the Apocalypse reveals an interesting set of parts and counterparts: *promises made* in Revelation 2–3 and *promises realized* in chapters 20–22. In the early chapters the risen Lord gives specific pledges that John's last vision, that of the New Jerusalem, sees fulfilled. For example, Jesus promised in Revelation 2:7, " 'To him who overcomes I will give the right to eat from the tree of life, which is in the paradise of God.' " In John's vision of paradise restored, he sees that the servants of God have free access to the tree of life within the holy city. He writes:

On each side of the river stood the tree of life, bearing twelve crops of fruit, yielding its fruit every month. And the leaves of the tree are for the healing of the nations (Rev. 22:2).

The Apocalypse's "promises made—promises realized" structure clearly indicates that time-wise, the book's content moves from the present to the future. It begins with the risen Jesus as our Priest-King (Rev. 1:12-18) and then moves to His glorious return and the restoration of paradise lost (19:11-21; 21:1-5). This forward movement makes the Revelation end-oriented.

There are other major correspondences of part and counterpart between the two halves of the Apocalypse. All seven promises to the churches in chapters 2–3 find their fulfillment in the New Jerusalem vision. Both main divisions of the Apocalypse speak about deliverance from the "second death" (Rev. 2:11; 20:6; 21:8), about receiving Jesus as the "morning star" (2:28; 22:16), about believers' names written in "the book of life" (3:5; 20:12, 15), about the name of God written on people's foreheads (3:12; 22:4), and about reigning with God forever and ever (3:21; 22:5). In short, "what the letters promised to the members of the churches is fulfilled in the citizens of the New Jerusalem according to Revelation 21–22. . . . What Jesus promised to the earthly church will be realized, definitively, in the Holy City."[1]

So, the seven letters to the church cannot be divorced from the rest of the book, as if Revelation 4–22 do not belong to the church. The deliberate correspondences between the first and the last chapters demonstrate that the Apocalypse is an indivisible unit and that to fully understand one part of the book one must relate it to its counterpart. The first division of the book anticipates the second part. This accounts for the clear progression of time between the two divisions of the book. It conveys the comforting message that God assures His faithful ones of their safe arrival in the New Jerusalem.

We find another example of the Apocalypse's forward movement in the correspondence between *justice requested* in the seals (Rev. 6:10) and *justice accomplished.* Note for instance the songs of triumph that shout:

"Hallelujah! Salvation and glory and power belong to our God, for true and just are his judgments. He *has* condemned the great prostitute who corrupted the earth with her adulteries.

He *has* avenged on her the blood of his servants" (Rev. 19:1, 2).

Chapter 20, with its millennial kingdom in heaven, shows how the martyrs are vindicated and rewarded with authority to judge (see verse 4). The fact that the millennium chapter has been placed in the second division of the Apocalypse shows that we're to understand that the millennium is a part of the future blessing.

The final parallel arrangement in the Apocalypse is that of the seven trumpet judgments in the first division of the book and the seven bowl plagues in the second. These two prophetic series of judgments succeed each other, with the seventh trumpet being disclosed as comprising the seven last plagues. The first six trumpets are limited in scope; they extend to only one third of the earth. Their purpose is to lead humankind to repentance and to turn to God. The seven last plagues, on the other hand, are worldwide and fall solely on the last generation of the wicked, after the close of probation (see Rev. 15:1-8). This arrangement confirms that the first six trumpet judgments proceed throughout church history, while the last plagues introduce Jesus' second advent. The gradual increase in intensity of God's response to human evil reveals His merciful character. He is reluctant to pour out His full wrath on sinners, restraining His chastisements that all may have time to repent and be saved.

What then is the meaning of the central branch of the Apocalypse, the middle part of the book, around which all the series of sevens are placed—that is, of chapters 10–14? This central part of the Apocalypse requires our careful attention.

Spotlight on the End Time: Revelation 10–14

No part of the Apocalypse is more relevant for the church today than John's visions in chapters 10–14. These visions are attached to the sixth trumpet in chapter 9 by way of an enlargement of that end-time period. Chapters 10–14 direct the beacon light of prophecy to the end-time church *before* the seventh trumpet sounds and the time of human probation ends.

The first two chapters of this section (Rev. 10, 11) introduce the heart of the book and foreshadow its content. This signals that a new story is about to be told. Chapter 10 begins with the appearance of a "mighty angel." This angel is authorized to announce the beginning of the time of the end and to commission a people to proclaim the gospel in the unique end-time setting. At the center of the vision stands a small scroll that has been opened, which indicates that an increased knowledge from the prophetic Word will be granted to the end-time church, with a new responsibility to make it known.

Let us look at the vision in Revelation 10:

> I saw another mighty angel coming down from heaven. He was robed in a cloud, with a rainbow above his head; his face was like the sun, and his legs were like fiery pillars. He was holding *a little scroll, which lay open* [Greek: *"having been opened"*] *in his hand.* He planted his right foot on the sea and his left foot on the land, and he gave a loud shout like the roar of a lion. . . . Then the angel I had seen standing on the sea and on the land raised his right hand to heaven. And *he swore by him who lives for ever and ever*, who created the heavens and all that is in them, the earth and all that is in it, and the sea and all that is in it, and said, *"There will be no more delay* [Greek: *chronos, "time"*—"There should be time no longer" (KJV)]! But in the days when the seventh angel is about to sound his trumpet, the mystery of God will be accomplished, just as he announced to his servants the prophets" (Rev. 10:1-3, 5-7).

When this vision comes to pass, the events leading to the end will be irrevocably set into motion. One leading Roman Catholic exegete, André Feuillet, acknowledged the specific end-time setting of Revelation 10 with these significant words:

> We feel compelled to conclude from this passage of the Apocalypse [Rev. 10:6, 7] that the history of salvation is in its last stage, the one immediately preceding the sound of the seventh trumpet.[2]

This end-time revelation for the church is at the heart of the entire Apocalypse. In choosing the concentric pattern of a menorah, the author makes the scroll of prophecy in chapters 10–14 the climactic center of its message. How eager then Christians should be to understand Jesus' final message for His church!

Revelation 10 portrays a heavenly messenger with messianic characteristics, like a Prince of light. His appearance resembles that of God when He came in the cloud on Mount Sinai with thunder and lightning to lead His people to the Promised Land. The little scroll that lies opened in his hand reveals a new commission for the church, based on her increased knowledge of the plan of God. Daniel's book concluded with this remarkable command and prediction: " 'But you, Daniel, close up and seal the words of the scroll until the time of the end. Many will go here and there to increase knowledge' " (12:4). The *opened* scroll suggests a direct connection with the scroll of Daniel, the only book that had been closed and sealed till the time of the end. What God closed and sealed He alone can unseal and open! So John's vision of Revelation 10 corresponds precisely with Daniel's prophecy.

This connection is confirmed by the similar oath sworn by the two messengers:

Daniel 12:7	Revelation 10:5, 6
The man clothed in linen, who was above the waters of the river, lifted his right hand and his left hand toward heaven, and I heard him *swear by him who lives forever*, saying, "*It will be for a time, times and half a time.* When the power of the holy people has been finally broken, all these things will be completed" (emphasis added).	Then the angel I had seen standing on the sea and on the land raised his right hand to heaven. And *he swore by him who lives for ever and ever*, who created the heavens and all that is in them, the earth and all that is in it, and the sea and all that is in it, and said, "*There will be no more delay* [Greek: *chronos*, "time"]!" (emphasis added).

The angel's oath in Revelation 10 marks a definite progress in time since the angel's oath in Daniel 12. The sixth trumpet announces that the three and a half prophetic "times" of Daniel have expired. In this sense there are no more prophetic times and thus no more delay! The time of the end has begun. This means that the *opened* scroll of Revelation 10 imparts a progressive understanding of Daniel's prophecies. Revelation 10 reveals what Daniel was unable to understand (Dan. 12:8). John indicates that the little scroll will be opened during the sixth trumpet. It remains open with a special end-time mission for the church: that of proclaiming an urgent message from the Creator to all peoples in the world.

A symbolic act that John performed portrays this task of the end-time church. A heavenly voice commanded John: " 'Go, take the scroll that lies open in the hand of the angel who is standing on the sea and on the land. . . . *Take it and eat it.* It will turn your stomach sour, but in your mouth it will be as sweet as honey' " (Rev. 10:8, 9, emphasis added). John received an explanation of this symbolic act immediately: "Then I was told, 'You must prophesy again about many peoples, nations, languages and kings' " (10:11).

Israel's prophets were familiar with symbolic actions. God asked some of them to use such techniques to deliver messages from Him (see Jer. 15:16, 17; and Ezek. 3:1-3). Israel's prophets had also experienced the sweet taste of assimilating God's message and the sour experience of proclaiming it publicly. They tasted the Word of God with joy, but when their message was rejected and opposed by false prophets, they experienced the bitterness of resistance. So, Revelation 11 offers a preview of the bitter resistance to Jesus' witnesses.

The commission to "prophesy again" about the destiny of the world during the sixth trumpet period announces a new initiative of God in the time of the end: the last warning message that lays bare the world's apostasy from its Creator and announces the approaching return of Jesus! The pertinent question is What particular message does God reveal to His end-time church in the book of Revelation? The answer is presented in the subsequent visions in chapters 12–14, which unfold the meaning of the scroll of Daniel.

The vision of Revelation 10 does not reveal the content of the end-time message. It intends only to remind people of their accountability to the Creator of the cosmos. This chapter introduces God's last message, which chapters 12–14 explicate. The message itself is found in 14:6-20, the three angels' messages. What Revelation 10 doesn't tell us about the new commission chapters 12–14 do.

The Structure of Revelation 12–14

Chapters 12–14 comprise an indivisible unit in which each chapter expands upon the content of the previous one, with an increasing focus on the end-time church. The following chart gives a brief overview of these central chapters and how they relate to each other:

Revelation 12	Revelation 13	Revelation 14
The dragon wages war against the woman of God (1-5).		
The woman flees into the wilderness for 1,260 days or 3½ times (6, 14).	The dragon employs a sea beast to make war against the saints and to conquer them for forty-two months (1-7).	
The dragon wages war against the rest of her offspring—"those who obey God's commandments and hold to the testimony of Jesus" (17).	A land beast emerges that supports the sea beast by enforcing its worship through a *mark of the beast* on a global scale (13-18).	The threefold message of 14:6-12 creates a faithful church that refuses the *mark of the beast*, because her saints "keep the commandments of God and the faith of Jesus" (12, RSV).

In the column that summarizes Revelation 12 we see three distinct phases in the history of the Christian church. The first phase was that of the early church, which the Roman Empire persecuted. A Roman governor prosecuted and crucified Jesus, and the cruel emperor Nero, whom many Christians of that time were convinced was the predicted antichrist, executed the apostles Peter and Paul.

The emperor Domitian banished the apostle John to Patmos. *Foxe's Book of Martyrs* says that the Roman authorities branded the Christians "atheists" and imputed to them every disaster, natural or otherwise, to justify torturing and executing them.

The church historian Eusebius tells the moving story of Polycarp, the old bishop of Smyrna. He was led into the stadium and given a chance to recant his Christian faith and save his life. The Roman proconsul asked the bishop, "What harm is it to say, 'Lord Caesar,' and to sacrifice, and to save yourself?" Polycarp answered, "Eighty-six years have I served Christ, and he never once wronged me; how then shall I blaspheme my King, who has saved me?"[3]

Some have estimated that perhaps three million Christians perished under the Roman emperors. In spite of this, many persevered in their faith and witnessed to the Word of God and the gospel of Jesus, and the early church survived.

The second phase of church history in Revelation 12 is that of the dark Middle Ages, during which so-called heretics and witches were outlawed, prosecuted, and executed by the state-church union for the crime of "heresy." This dreadful period lasted more than a thousand years. In Revelation 12 it is called the "1,260 days" or the "time, times, and half a time" (during which the "woman" of God hid in the wilderness [Rev, 12:6, 14]). A shocking example is the massacre of the Huguenots in France that began on St. Bartholomew's Day, August 24, 1572. On that day more than seventy thousand Protestants were murdered at the command of a king and his mother, Catharine de Medici, who acted under the direction of the papacy. Pope Gregory XIII struck a special medal to commemorate his triumph in "the massacre of the Huguenots." Nevertheless, a remnant of followers of Jesus continued to witness courageously to the Word of God and the testimony of Jesus, as Revelation 6:9 predicted.

The third phase is that of the remnant church of Jesus. She again stands firmly on the solid platform of the apostolic faith: the commandments of God and the testimony of Jesus (see Rev. 12:17). These two fundamental beliefs are the abiding hallmark of the true saints of God in all ages. (For an in-depth treatment, see Appendix C.)

The Sea Beast and the Land Beast

Looking at the second column, we observe that Revelation 13 shows two evil powers that emerge as agents of the dragon; namely, the sea beast and the land beast. The unholy alliance of the dragon and these two beasts forms a satanic trinity.

Significant links between chapters 12 and 13 indicate their parallel arrangement. The first connecting link is the time symbol for the period of persecution: 42 months in chapter 13:5, and 1,260 days or three and a half "times" in chapter 12:6, 14. The second link is the war against the saints. Chapter 12 refers to two major periods of warfare against the saints: the one against the woman in the wilderness (Rev. 12:6), and the final war against the saints (12:17). Chapter 13 enlarges on these two wars of the dragon by revealing that the dragon will enlist the aid of the sea beast and the land beast.

Looking at the third column, we notice that Revelation 14 focuses strictly on the final attack of the antichrist against the saints. This chapter reveals God's counteroffensive against the antichrist's final thrust and exhorts His people to resist the beast and to reject its mark of allegiance.

Let us look closely at two corresponding passages: Rev. 13:15-17 and 14:9-11. A comparison of both passages reveals that they present two sides of the same coin: first the dark side, then the bright one. The two visions complement and clarify each other, and neither can be fully understood without the other:

Revelation 13:15-17	Revelation 14:9-11
He [the land beast] was given power to give breath to the image of the first beast [the sea beast], so that it could speak and cause all who refused to worship the image to be killed. He also forced everyone, small and great, rich and poor, free and slave, to receive a *mark* on his right hand or on his forehead, so that no one could buy	A third angel followed them and said in a loud voice: "If anyone worships the beast and his image and receives his *mark* on the forehead or on the hand, he, too, will drink of the wine of God's fury, which has been poured full strength into the cup of his wrath. . . . There is no rest day or night for those who worship the beast and his image,

Revelation 13:15-17	Revelation 14:9-11
or sell unless he had the *mark*, which is the name of the beast or the number of his name (emphasis added).	or for anyone who receives the *mark* of his name" (emphasis added).

This comparison proves that Revelation 13 and 14 run parallel to each other, with chapter 14 offering an increasing focus on the end-time test of faith.

Equally important is the parallelism of the verses in Revelation 12 and 14 that depict Jesus' end-time church. Again we detect a clarification in the final vision:

Revelation 12:17	Revelation 14:12 (RSV)
The dragon was enraged at the woman and went off to make war against the rest of her offspring— *those who obey God's commandments and hold to the testimony of Jesus* (emphasis added).	Here is a call for the endurance of the saints, *those who keep the commandments of God and the faith of Jesus* (emphasis added).

Both end-time passages identify the faithful saints as those who obey the commandments of God and hold to the testimony of Jesus. Significantly, Revelation 14:12 clarifies chapter 12:17's "the testimony of Jesus" as "the faith of Jesus." The "faith of Jesus" is an explanatory equivalent of "the testimony of Jesus." That means that the testimony of Jesus is the historic faith or teaching of Jesus as reported in the New Testament. This "testimony of Jesus" also includes the book of Revelation, which the risen Lord called His "testimony for the churches" (Rev. 22:16).

Jude, Jesus' brother, urged the church "to contend for the faith that was once for all entrusted to the saints" (Jude 3). The content of this apostolic faith was: "the Word of God [or the commandments of God] and the testimony [or the faith] of Jesus" (Rev. 1:2), as represented by the two authoritative witnesses: the Old and the New Testaments. Earlier, Paul wrote that the "holy Scriptures" were sufficient "for salvation through faith in Christ Jesus" (2 Tim. 3:15). The last generation of God's people will restore the essential truths of both Testaments in their worship of God, in contrast with the worldwide apostasy from the Creator-Redeemer.

In summary, the literary linkages between chapters 12, 13, and 14 demonstrate that these visions do not teach a chronological sequence but are parallel outlines of church history that intend to clarify each other with a sharpening focus on the final phase of history. The prophetic spotlight focuses on God's people in their final confrontation with the antichrist.

The Cross: Central Theme of the Apocalypse

Revelation 12 shows that the bitter warfare against the saints on earth was initiated by Satan "who leads the whole world astray" (Rev. 12:9). This hostility against Jesus' people is the aftermath of a cosmic war between Satan and God (see 12:7-9). The Son of God has defeated Satan and thrown him down to the earth, sealing his downfall by His redemptive work on the cross. Heaven itself proclaims the cosmic significance of Jesus' historic triumph over Satan:

> "Now have come the salvation and the power and the kingdom of our God, and the authority of his Christ. For the accuser of our brothers, who accuses them before our God day and night, has been hurled down" (Rev. 12:10).

Jesus knew that His atoning death would result in Satan's expulsion from heaven. He announced: " 'Now is the time for judgment on this world; now the prince of this world will be driven out' " (John 12:31). So Jesus won the war against Satan on behalf of all humankind! All the hostility the saints experience must be viewed in the light of Satan's war against Jesus. Ellen G. White made this spiritual dimension crystal clear:

> The great conflict now being waged is not merely a strife of man against man. On one side stands the Prince of life, acting as man's substitute and surety; on the other, the prince of dark-

ness, with the fallen angels under his command.[4]

Satan is now a defeated enemy! And Christians may participate in Jesus' victory by faith in Him and by obeying His testimony till the end:

"They overcame him by the blood of the Lamb and by the word of their testimony; they did not love their lives so much as to shrink from death" (Rev. 12:11).

The central vision of Revelation 12:7-12 demonstrates that the gospel of Jesus is the controlling theme of the Apocalypse. It provides unshakable assurance that God will reestablish His rule, His kingdom, on earth.

---

1. Roberto Badenas, in *Symposium on Revelation*, Frank B. Holbrook, ed. (Silver Spring, Md.: Biblical Research Institute, 1992), Book II, 264, 265.
2. André Feuillet, *Johannine Studies*, (New York: Alba House, 1966), 220.
3. See *Foxe's Book of Martyrs* (Grand Rapids, Mich.: Baker Books, 1995), 21, 22.
4. Ellen G. White, *Review and Herald*, Feb. 6, 1900; quoted in the Seventh-day Adventist Bible Commentary, Vol. 7:974, 975.

Chapter Five

HOW TO INTERPRET REVELATION'S PROPHETIC LANGUAGE

The Book of Revelation possesses a distinctively Hebrew character. The reason for its Hebraic nature is clear: while the author, John, writes in Greek, he thinks in Hebrew! John was intimately acquainted with the Hebrew text of the Old Testament; he alludes to it more than six hundred times. He apparently did his own translating from the Hebrew text because he never quotes from any Greek version. And although he does not cite directly from the Scriptures, he continually adopts the language of the Old Testament prophets. He places their images in a new setting: that of the gospel of Jesus Christ. More than any other book of the New Testament, the Apocalypse emphasizes the glory of the risen Christ. "Many designations that belong alone to God in the Old Testament are freely used of Christ."[1] Revelation thus gives the Hebrew passages a developed meaning, a Christ-centered interpretation.

John's Apocalypse unites the essence of the two Testaments by honoring both the God of Israel and the deity of Jesus Christ. The book presupposes the Gospels and the Letters of the New Testament. One may even say "in the Revelation all the books of the Bible meet and end."[2] The Apocalypse is unique in that it shows how the other books of the Bible find their ultimate fulfillment at the end of this age. To put it another way, Revelation says that Israel's history will essentially be repeated and brought to a worldwide consummation in the people of Christ.

The fact that the last Bible book sums up the theological message of both the Old and the New Testaments provides two inspired keys to unlocking its symbolic language. The first key is the Hebrew Bible. Whenever John refers to the Old Testament, he establishes a spiritual correspondence between Israel and the church of Christ. Paul calls it a relationship of type and antitype (1 Cor. 10:6, 11). This means that God's covenant with Israel is a prefiguration or foreshadowing of His better covenant with Christian believers—that is, with the messianic people of God. The Letter to the Hebrews assures us that "Jesus has become the guarantee of a better covenant" (7:22).

This points to the second key to unlocking the Hebrew terms and images of the Apocalypse: the gospel of Jesus Christ. Without this second key many today are forced to literalize all the Hebrew terms and names in the Apocalypse and then to apply them to the Jewish people and to their land in the Middle East. This method of understanding the prophetic language is called *literalism*. It shifts the focus of prophecy away from Jesus to the Jews of today and to their politics. However, God's covenant promises are not primarily Israel-centered but Christ-centered! The messianic prophecies are the heart of God's covenant with Israel (Pss. 2; 110).

All Scripture Testifies of Jesus

Jesus brought this messianic focus of Scripture to the attention of the Jewish leaders when He said:

"You diligently study the Scriptures because you think that by them you possess eternal life. These are the Scriptures that testify about me, yet you refuse to come to me to have life. . . . If you believed Moses, you would believe me, for he wrote about me. But since you do not believe what he wrote, how are you going to believe what I say?" (John 5:39, 40, 46, 47).

Even Jesus' own disciples had to be reoriented to the messianic center of the Scriptures because their minds were so focused on Israel (see Acts 1:6). After His resurrection from the dead, Jesus reproved them:

"How foolish you are, and how slow of heart to believe all that the prophets have spoken! Did not the Christ have to suffer these things and then enter his glory?" And beginning with Moses and all the Prophets, he explained to them what was said in all the Scriptures concerning himself (Luke 24:25-27).

After the outpouring of the Holy Spirit at Pentecost, the apostles learned their lesson. No longer was their gospel message centered in Israel or the Middle East, but exclusively in Jesus and His redemptive work on our behalf (1 Cor. 15:1-5). Paul quotes a central covenant promise: " 'Everyone who calls on the name of the Lord will be saved' " (Rom. 10:13; from Joel 2:32). He applied this divine promise to all who call on the name of the Lord Jesus (see Rom. 10:9). This is the salvation-historical advance from the old to the new covenant. This change marks the basic difference between Christianity and Judaism.

Jesus and His apostles adopted the Hebrew Scriptures as the foundation of their gospel. The first Christians saw the two Testaments as two witnesses of the same God, who in His Son continued salvation history from promise to fulfillment, from type to antitype, from shadow to reality. The risen Lord Jesus built His Apocalypse on this apostolic testimony. He provided His struggling church with a new truth from the God of Israel that would encourage His followers to persevere and to renew their hope in the kingdom of God.

One scholar says of Revelation:

> The chief theme . . . is not what God in Christ has done for the world, but what He will yet do, and what the assured consummation will be. It is therefore the Gospel of faith and hope, and seeks to inspire the Churches anew in these respects; for that the end is nigh.[3]

John provided a new perspective on the future of God's covenant people. His instructions were: " 'Write, therefore, what you have seen, what is now and what will take place later' " (Rev. 1:19). In other words, his book begins with the apostolic church and proceeds through the post-apostolic church until the end of this age. "This revelation was given for the guidance and comfort of the church throughout the Christian dispensation."[4] No other book in the Bible fills this need more sublimely.

Using Both Keys

The method of deriving the message God intended the church to receive from Revelation's Hebrew images is critical. It requires the use of both the interpretative keys that the book itself gives. Only then can we be sure that speculative ideas are not adulterating our interpretation of the visions.

Revelation begins with these significant words:

"The revelation of Jesus Christ, which God gave him to show his servants what must soon take place" (1:1).

So God is the source of the visions. But what God is in view? Undoubtedly the God of Israel, the God of the Hebrew prophets (see Heb. 1:1, 2). It's the covenant God of Israel who has acted in the life and mission of Jesus Christ. He wants to assure both Jews and Christians that His plan for the redemption of the world will not fail and that His covenant with Israel will be fulfilled beyond all human expectations in the New Jerusalem on the earth made new. The emphasis here is on the essential continuity of God's promises and on their glorious consummation.

Regarding verse 1, the margins of most versions refer to Daniel 2:28 to indicate a connection with the prophet Daniel. This connection is significant:

Daniel 2:28	Revelation 1:1
"There is a God in heaven who reveals mysteries. He has shown King Nebuchadnezzar what will happen in *days to come* [Greek: *dei genesthai ep' eschatôn tôn hêmerôn*]."	God gave him to show what must *soon* take place [Greek: *dei genesthai en tachei*].

God showed future events to both Daniel and John by means of visions. And a continuity exists between their visions. What Daniel foretold Nebuchadnezzar, king of Babylon, more than five hundred years before Christ becomes an urgent theme in the book of Revelation. However, what Daniel predicted for the distant future and sealed until "the time of the end" (Dan. 12:4) John was told will "soon take place." In other words, the time of fulfillment has advanced. With Jesus' death and resurrection, the events Daniel predicted have moved closer to their end-time realization! So, in contrast with Daniel, John was ordered: " 'Do not seal up the words of the prophecy of this book, because the time is near' " (Rev. 22:10). This means that the book of Revelation is a progressive interpretation of Daniel's visions.

Obviously, then, we must study both books together. In this relationship Daniel functions as the root and Revelation as the fruit. To understand the prophetic language of the book of Revelation, the Christian must use both inspired keys: the Old Testament and the gospel. John points to these as follows:

"Who testified to the word of God and to the testimony of Jesus Christ, even to all that he saw" (Rev. 1:2, NRSV).

The twofold phrase, "the word of God and the testimony of Jesus Christ," represents the two authoritative revelations of God to His covenant people. It unites God's word through the Hebrew prophets with the testimony that Jesus gave through the Spirit of prophecy in the New Testament (see John 3:34; 12:48; Heb. 1:1, 2). Thus, the Apocalypse unites both Testaments, creatively showing the essential continuity of God's plan of redemption in Jesus. John repeated this point by stating that he was banished to Patmos "because of the word of God and the testimony of Jesus" (Rev. 1:9). This progressive unity of both Testaments was an essential part of the apostolic faith!

John placed the central theme of the Apocalypse at the beginning:

> Look, he is coming with the clouds,
>   and every eye will see him,
> even those who pierced him;
>   and all the peoples of the earth will mourn because of him.
>   So shall it be! Amen.
>   "I am the Alpha and the Omega," says the Lord God, "who is,
> and who was, and who is to come, the Almighty" (Rev. 1:7, 8).

To receive the full impact of this assurance, we must trace its roots in the Hebrew Scriptures. Most Bible margins refer to Daniel 7:13 and Zechariah 12:10. That means that we are witnessing in Revelation 1:7 the phenomenon of a blending of different Hebrew passages to show their fulfillment in Jesus. The Apocalypse focuses on the consummation of Israel's covenant promises at Jesus' second coming. Revelation 1:7 states the great goal to which all visions lead. Let us take a careful look at John's second use of Daniel in Revelation.

Daniel 7:13	Revelation 1:7
"In my vision at night I looked, and there before me was one like a son of man, *coming with the clouds of heaven.* He approached the Ancient of Days and was led into his presence" (emphasis added).	Look, *he is coming with the clouds,* and every eye will see him, even those who pierced him; and all the peoples of the earth will mourn because of him. So shall it be! Amen (emphasis added).

Revelation 1:7 presents a clear reference to Daniel 7:13. Its purpose is not to offer a literal exegesis of this passage in the Old

Testament context, but to disclose a further fulfillment of Daniel 7 in the second advent of Jesus. To understand John's messianic application of Daniel's prophecy, we must go back to Daniel to learn his own prophetic perspective. It is essential for the correct understanding of the last Bible book to place Daniel's visions behind the developed visions of John.

Daniel: the Inspired Chronologist

Daniel lived during the Neo-Babylonian Empire (605-539 B.C.). He first described a vision that God gave to king Nebuchadnezzar. That emperor had seen a statue made of four metals: a golden head, silver breast and arms, bronze belly and thighs, legs of iron, and feet made of a mixture of iron and clay. Then a movement caught the prophet's eye: "A rock was cut out, but *not by human hands*. It struck the statue on its feet of iron and clay and smashed them" (Dan. 2:34). The rock itself then became a huge mountain and filled the whole earth (v. 35). Daniel explained that the four metallic parts of the statue represent four successive empires that would rule the world, beginning with Babylon (see vs. 36-40). After the fourth world empire would come "a divided kingdom," partly strong and partly brittle, that would "not remain united" (vs. 41-43).

Daniel reached the high point of his vision when he predicted that

> "in the time of those kings, the God of heaven will set up a kingdom that will never be destroyed, nor will it be left to another people. It will crush all those kingdoms and bring them to an end, but it will itself endure forever" (Dan. 2:44).

So, Daniel 2 presents a divine forecast in which God portrays the outcome of world history. This chapter portrays history from a secular viewpoint, one that would appeal to an Oriental despot. Conservative Bible scholars sometimes call the prophecy of Daniel 2 the ABCs of apocalyptic prophecy. It introduces a pattern that Daniel's prophecies repeat—that of presenting a sequence of coming kingdoms. This pattern shows a succession of ever-weakening rulerships until the God of heaven intervenes in human affairs to establish His own eternal kingdom on earth.

The standard conservative application of the four metal parts of the statue to history finds the fulfillment in Babylon, Medo-Persia, Greece, and Rome. John's Apocalypse adopted this interpretation (see chapters 12, 13), and so did the church fathers. The Roman Empire lasted as a political unity until A.D. 476. Since then, the world has never again been united under one head despite repeated efforts to establish a new world empire by military might or through intermarriage of royal families. The efforts of Justinian, Charles the Great, Napoleon, and Hitler all failed. Some twenty-five hundred years have passed since God gave His forecast through Daniel. Every detail has been fulfilled in history with surprising accuracy. No dictator has ever successfully refuted these few words of prophecy: "Just as you saw that the feet and toes were partly of baked clay and partly of iron, so this will be a divided kingdom" (Dan. 2:41). Today we see that according to Daniel 2, we are living near the end of world history.

The parallel between the second and the seventh chapters of Daniel is clear. Daniel 7 also portrays the four world empires, but now as they appear as ravenous beasts in their hostility to God's people. The prophet saw four wild animals emerge from the turbulent sea, one after the other: a winged lion, a hungry bear, a winged leopard with four heads, and finally, a terrible beast with iron teeth and ten horns that "crushed and devoured its victims" (Dan. 7:7).

The most striking revelation, however, was that another horn would begin to grow among the ten horns of the beast, until it dominated all the others and uprooted three of them. Daniel focused on this "little" horn, providing some details of its audacious religious claims and its cruel warfare against the saints of God (Dan. 7:20, 24, 25). He pictured the emergence of the antichrist *after* the dissolution of the Roman Empire and predicted its successful long-term domination over the faithful worshipers of God. More importantly, Daniel also assured the saints that God will eventually vindicate their cause and bring His righteous judgment on their cruel enemy:

As I watched, this horn was waging war against the saints and defeating them, *until the Ancient of Days came and pronounced judgment in favor of the saints of the Most High*, and the time came when they possessed the kingdom (Dan. 7:21, 22, emphasis added).

In this prophecy Daniel disclosed that in His providence God allows the "little horn" to persecute the believers right down to the close of probation and the coming of His kingdom. But God will have the last word, and it will be in favor of the saints! This divine assurance restores full confidence in the providential rule of the Most High.

Some characteristics of the antichrist deserve our special attention:

"He will speak against the Most High and oppress the saints and try to change the set times and the laws. The saints will be handed over to him for a time, times and half a time" (Dan. 7:25).

The three and a half "times" of persecution are mentioned once again in Daniel 12:7 and return in the book of Revelation in synonymous expressions as "1,260 days" or "42 months" (Rev. 12:6, 14; 13:5). This time-symbol definitely links Daniel's visions with those of John. Consequently, we cannot interpret the language of Revelation without considering Daniel's apocalyptic visions. Daniel was the apocalyptic chronologist. His outline provided the framework for John's prophecy of church history. Significantly, John's vision of the rise and fall of the sea beast in chapter 13 builds on and adds to that of the little horn in Daniel 7. John combines the features of the four beasts and those of the little horn in one composite beast:

I saw a beast coming out of the sea. He had ten horns and seven heads, with ten crowns on his horns, and on each head a blasphemous name. The beast I saw resembled a leopard, but had feet like those of a bear and a mouth like that of a lion (Rev. 13:1, 2).

The connection of Revelation 13 with Daniel 7 is of decisive importance. Both use the same symbolic images, but Revelation pictures world history from the viewpoint of a later date. The new revelation is that John sees the ten horns "with ten crowns," suggesting a definite progress in time beyond the Roman Empire. John lived in the time of the fourth beast, the Roman Empire—when Daniel's first three world empires had expired. And John's prophetic language points to a stage of history farther down the line: to the time when the "ten horns" have their "crowns" and therefore rule in place of the Roman Empire (Dan. 7:24; Rev. 13:1). Only in that epoch of history will the persecuting little horn arise "among" the ten kingdoms (Dan. 7:8). So, Revelation 13 enlarges Daniel 7 and focuses specifically on the persecuting power of the little horn:

The Little Horn Daniel 7	The Sea Beast Revelation 13
"He will speak against the Most High and oppress his saints. . . . The saints will be handed over to him for a time, times and half a time" (verse 25).	The beast was given a mouth to utter proud words and blasphemies and to exercise his authority for forty-two months. . . . He was given power to make war against the saints and to conquer them (verses 5, 7).

John's vision of the antichrist-beast, then, expands Daniel's vision of the little horn. Revelation 13 presents an inspired application of Daniel 7 for the church age. This understanding was the prevalent interpretation in the Reformation churches of Europe and North America for more than three hundred years.[5]

Progressive Application of the Prophetic Language

We also see evidences of Revelation's close connection with Daniel in John's description of his cardinal theme: "Look, he is coming with the clouds, and every eye will see him, even those who pierced him" (Rev. 1:7). Taken by itself, this statement does not release its profound meaning and impact. Daniel 7:13, 14 holds the key to unlocking its significance.

"In my vision at night I looked, and there before me was *one like a son of man, coming with the clouds of heaven. He approached the Ancient of Days and was led into his presence.* He was given authority, glory and sovereign power; all peoples, nations and men of every language worshiped him. His dominion is an everlasting dominion that will not pass away, and his kingdom is one that will never be destroyed."

Daniel's vision of the appearance of a celestial Deliverer becomes the main theme of John's Apocalypse. The entire vision of Daniel 7 stands behind John's Apocalypse as its original setting.

Daniel saw a human-like Being carried by a "cloud" or "chariot" of angels to the Most High, from Whom He then received the authority to share His rulership with the saints forever (see Dan. 7:27). Because this heavenly Being resembles a human being, Daniel described Him as "one like a son of man." But in reality He is the unique Son of God, far exalted above all angels (see Matt. 26:64; Heb. 1:6-8).

The book of 1 Enoch, in its section entitled "Similitudes," dated by scholars in the first century of the Christian era, describes a vision about an individual who was with God and who had a face "like that of a human being." This pre-existent Messiah sits in heaven on His throne of glory and passes judgment upon all mortal and spiritual beings. An angel explains: " 'This is the Son of Man, to whom belongs righteousness. . . . He shall depose the kings from their thrones and kingdoms. For they do not extol and glorify him, and neither do they obey him, the source of their kingship.' "[6] The book of 1 Enoch was familiar to the writers of the New Testament. (Jude 14, 15 even cites 1 Enoch 1:9.) This Jewish writing interpreted the vision of Daniel 7 as a messianic prophecy. The surprise for the Jewish readers of John's Apocalypse was that this celestial "son of man" in Daniel 7 was the risen Lord Jesus!

While Daniel saw that the Messiah was led "with the clouds of heaven" to the Ancient of Days in heaven, John described a subsequent stage in Jesus' ministry: His coming "with the clouds" from heaven to the earth! John developed Daniel 7:13, 14 by reapplying Daniel's vision to Jesus' return to earth to deliver His followers. This new application shows a progression in salvation history. And Revelation 14:14, in which John expanded his portrayal of the second advent of Jesus, repeats this advancement:

"I looked, and there before me was a white cloud, and seated on the cloud was one *'like a son of man'* with a crown of gold on his head and a sharp sickle in his hand."

This description of Jesus shows that John was not citing Jesus' claim to be "the Son of Man" (which appears 77 times in the Gospels). Rather, he took the phrase "one *like* a son of man" directly from Daniel 7:13! Here's another evidence that John wrote his Apocalypse with the Hebrew text of Daniel in front of him. John wanted to disclose what Jesus will do after His investiture as King-Judge in Daniel 7. Thus Revelation complements, explains, and unfolds Daniel's book.

In Revelation 1 John added to his vision of the returning Jesus: "Every eye will see him, even those who pierced him" (Rev. 1:7). These words are a direct reference to words in Zechariah 12:10. Writing more than five hundred years before the Christian era, the prophet Zechariah predicted that Jerusalem would "pierce" or kill her God-sent Messiah and that many would grieve bitterly about their part in that evil deed:

"I will pour out on the house of David and the inhabitants of Jerusalem a spirit of grace and supplication. They will look on me, the one they have pierced, and they will mourn for him as one mourns for an only child, and grieve bitterly for him as one grieves for a firstborn son" (Zech. 12:10).

The New Testament sheds light on Zechariah's mysterious prophecy. John refers to it more than once, each time with a decided Christo–centric application. The Gospel of John declares that Jesus died when a Roman soldier "pierced Jesus' side with a spear, bringing a sudden flow of blood and water" (John 19:34). John adds:

"These things happened so that the Scripture would be fulfilled: . . . 'They will look on the one they have pierced' " (vs. 36, 37). The shocking surprise for the Jews came, however, when John announced that *all* who "pierced" Jesus in some form or another will see Him coming as divine King and Judge. John added that at that time "all the peoples [Greek: *phylai*] of the earth will mourn because of him" (Rev. 1:7). This announcement gives Zechariah's prediction a dramatic, worldwide consummation involving all the rejecters of Jesus' lordship at His second coming.

John combined the messianic prophecies of Daniel and Zechariah in his own apocalyptic outlook. His language blends both Hebrew prophecies to emphasize the fulfillment of all Israel's hopes in the crucified and risen Lord Jesus. God's plan knows no failure and will soon receive its universal and cosmic fulfillment at the return of Jesus Christ. John demonstrates this purpose again in his vivid description in Revelation 19:11-15 of Jesus' coming as the Divine Warrior at Armageddon. Here John reveals that the risen Jesus will execute four Hebrew judgment visions, those of Psalm 2:9; Isaiah 11:4; 63:1-4; and Jeremiah 25:30-33.* Revelation 19's climactic vision serves to reassure us of the spiritual unity of the Old and the New Testaments and their covenants in the Lord Jesus.

While the New Testament proclaims *who* the Messiah is, the Old Testament explains *what* the Messiah's mission is all about. The Apocalypse has even been called (by André Feuillet) a "Christian re-reading of the Old Testament." No other book makes a more deliberate use of the Hebrew Scriptures than does John's Apocalypse. John demonstrates thereby *in what way* the God of Israel will consummate His promises and curses. The book of Revelation consistently presents a functional identification of Jesus with God, meaning that as God's representative He will carry out the divine function of judgment and salvation.

John concludes his glorious vision of Jesus with His assurance:

---

*For more on these connections, see my book *Chariots of Salvation: The Biblical Drama of Armageddon*, chapter 8.

" 'I am the Alpha and the Omega' " (Rev. 1:8). This is the Greek form of the title of Israel's covenant God, " 'I am the first and I am the last' " (Isa. 44:6). This title signifies God's sovereign lordship over history from the beginning till the end. John clarifies God's title by the additional words, " 'Who is, and who was, and who is to come, the Almighty [*Pantokratôr*]' " (Rev. 1:8). Here he points to God's pledge to come again to our planet to restore Paradise lost (see also 4:8; 11:17; 15:3; 16:7, 15; 21:22). God's promise guarantees that He will ultimately rule the world in righteousness and peace through Jesus Christ!

1. R. H. Charles, *The Revelation of St. John*, The International Critical Commentary (Edinburgh: T. & T. Clark, 1975), vol.1: cxii.
2. Ellen G. White, *The Acts of the Apostles* (Nampa, Idaho: Pacific Press, 1911), 585.
3. Charles, vol. 1:cix.
4. White, 583.
5. For documentation, see L. E. Froom, *The Prophetic Faith of Our Fathers* (Hagerstown, Md.: Review & Herald, 1948-1954), vols. 2–4.
6. 1 Enoch 46:3, in *The Old Testament Pseudepigrapha*, J. H. Charlesworth, ed. (New York: Doubleday, 1983), vol. 1:34.

Chapter Six

SPECIAL SPOTLIGHTS
ON
THE END TIME

A knowledge of the literary composition of the Apocalypse contributes considerably to our understanding of its message. The cycles of visions receive their meaning from the place they occupy in the structure of the book. John uses four cycles of sevens to give his work unity: the seven letters (Rev. 2, 3), the seven seals (Rev. 5, 6), the seven trumpets (Rev. 8, 9; 11:15-19), and the seven plagues (Rev. 15, 16). Each series of seven forms a complete unit of its own. And rather than comprising one long chronological sequence, the series (with the exception of the plagues) each cover the entire Christian era, each of them from a different viewpoint. In other words, the cycles supplement each other.

The use of seven items in these prophetic cycles signifies a continuous forward movement. This repeated forward thrust characterizes the Apocalypse as basically *end-oriented*. John introduced this Second-Coming orientation near the beginning of the book: "Look, he is coming with the clouds, and every eye will see him" (1:7).

Each series moves forward in time till it reaches the Day of

Judgment, so that the entire narrative of the Apocalypse repeatedly moves from promise to fulfillment. This pattern can be compared with a conical spiral or with a staircase that winds upward concentrically. This becomes evident when we compare Revelation's various end-time passages:

Revelation 6:16, 17 The Sixth Seal	Revelation 11:15 The Seventh Trumpet	Revelation 14:14 Conclusion of End Time	Revelation 19:11 The Seventh Plague
They called to the mountains . . . "Fall on us and hide us from the face of him who sits on the throne and from the wrath of the Lamb! For the great day of their wrath has come."	"The kingdom of the world has become the kingdom of our Lord and of his Christ, and he will reign forever and ever."	I looked, and there before me was a white cloud, and seated on the cloud was one "like a son of man" with a crown of gold on his head and a sharp sickle in his hand.	I saw heaven standing open and there before me was a white horse, whose rider is called Faithful and True. With justice he judges and makes war.

This alignment shows that the seals, the trumpets, the plagues, and the end-time message all climax in the Second Advent. So, John intended these cycles to serve as parallel forecasts that recapitulate the church age from different points of view. Especially noteworthy is the fact that the seals, trumpets, end-time messages, and plagues all contain an added vision that spotlights a particular end-time event. By means of these interludes, the Apocalypse emphasizes the final stage of world history. These end-time visions, inserted at the sixth seal, the sixth trumpet, the sixth plague, and at the last test of faith, intend to enlarge upon the preceding events in each chain for the benefit of God's people. These parenthetical visions, which C. Mervyn Maxwell called "scenes of end-time assignment and assurance," supply some of Revelation's most meaningful and reassuring messages (see chapters 7; 10; 11; 14:1-5; 16:15).

Jesus' Letters to the Churches

The terms in which Jesus introduces Himself to each church come from John's vision of Jesus' priestly ministry in heaven (Rev. 1:12-16). The seven letters, then, belong to John's vision of Jesus as Lord of the church. These letters speak on more than one level. First, they were addressed to particular church communities in Asia Minor at the end of the first century of the Christian Era. Second, Jesus' counsels and promises belong to each believer at any time, as indicated by the concluding words of every letter: "He who has an ear, let him hear what the Spirit says to the churches" (Rev. 2:7, 11, 17, etc.).

Third, some letters also point to the future. For instance, Jesus predicted that His followers in Smyrna would suffer a special persecution "for ten days" (2:10). Between A.D. 165 and 180, the church in Smyrna was severely persecuted and became the site of some notable martyrdoms, the most memorable of which was that of Polycarp, the aged bishop of Smyrna.[1]

Another predictive element is the promise to the church in Philadelphia: " 'Since you have kept my command to endure patiently, I will also keep you from the hour of trial that is going to come upon the whole world to test those who live on the earth' " (Rev. 3:10). Jesus' promise to "keep" His followers does not mean that He will remove them from the world. Instead, He is promising protection in the midst of the final suffering and persecution. John's vision of the "sealing" of the faithful ones (chapter 7) further develops this thought. The promises in the letters also show signs of increasing urgency regarding the Second Coming (see Rev. 2:16, 25; 3:3, 11, 20).

C. Mervyn Maxwell explains the abiding significance of the seven letters:

> Just as the letters applied to seven local churches at one time, and just as they apply to individuals everywhere and at all times, it is evident that they also apply to the various conditions of the church—that is, to the various conditions of congregations, denominations, and movements—at all times.[2]

We must not divorce the seven letters from the rest of the

Apocalypse. The book as a whole is a pastoral-prophetic letter directed to all churches. It shows a movement from the apostolic church (chapters 1–3) to the post-apostolic church through the centuries (chapters 12–14) until the saints arrive safely in the City of God (chapters 20–22).

The Seven-sealed Scroll

Revelation 4 conveys John's vision of the throne of God. Then, in chapter 5, he sees the Lamb of God taking a seven-sealed scroll from the right hand of the One who sits upon the throne. The image of the throne appears in the center of both these visions. The throne of God and Jesus functions as a key theme throughout the entire Apocalypse. So, because chapters 4 and 5 introduce this theme, they serve as the source for all the judgments and blessings that follow in later chapters.

The ultimate question is Who rules the world? Who is its legitimate King? The throne vision of chapter 5 answers that question. It validates Jesus' claim that He has conquered and now shares in God's power (Rev. 3:21). No created being in heaven or on earth has the worthiness of the risen Lord Jesus. He alone is acclaimed "worthy" to open the seals of the scroll the Father holds. This has far-reaching consequences for the subsequent visions of the Apocalypse.

John portrays Jesus as the Lamb who has "seven horns and seven eyes, which are the seven spirits of God sent out into all the earth" (Rev. 5:6). This symbolizes Jesus' fullness of power and wisdom to lead the world to its appointed end. The transfer of the sealed scroll from the Father to Jesus makes Him the Lord over planet Earth. He is named King of the world and Executor of God's decrees. Human history is placed in the hands of the risen Lord. With each seal He breaks on the scroll of destiny, He inaugurates a new phase in the history of the church—until the sixth seal reveals the terrible Day of Judgment for all who have rejected the kingship of the Lamb of God.

Understanding the Seven Seals

The seals of Revelation 6 show a surprising aspect of Jesus' reign.

They portray the persecution of Jesus' followers during the entire church age by the powers of the world. Placing the seal cycle beside Jesus' prophetic discourse in Matthew 24 confirms their coverage of the Christian Era. A comparison of the two prophetic sequences reveals that they both follow the same order of events and conclude with Jesus' second advent.

Matthew 24	Revelation 6 (Seals)
Warning against false christs (v. 5)	(I) White horse rider conquers
Local wars, rumors of wars (v. 6); international conflicts (v. 7)	(II) Red horse: brings wars
Famines and earthquakes (v. 7)	(III) Black horse: brings famines
Persecution and executions (v. 9); apostasy and false prophets (vs. 10, 11)	(IV) Pale horse: brings death through sword, famine, plague, and wild beasts.
Worldwide gospel preaching (v. 14); unequaled worldwide distress for the true Christians (vs. 21, 22)	(V) Martyred souls cry out for justice, but have to wait "a little longer."
Cosmic signs: sun, moon, stars (v. 29); the Son of Man appears in the sky, causing worldwide remorse (v. 30)	(VI) Cosmic signs, a great earthquake, causing worldwide fear for the wrath of the Lamb.

Obviously, the seals of Revelation 6 are an enlargement of Jesus' verbal sketch of the church age in Matthew 24. The seals disclose the extent of the long tribulation of the saints. The historical progression of the seals leads the cycle forward in time till it reaches the final judgment in the sixth seal.

In the past, God had sent four dreadful judgments—"sword and famine and wild beasts and plague" (Ezek. 14:21)—on His rebellious covenant people. But these judgments were not God's final judgment. They served as preliminary judgments—warnings to motivate His wayward people to return to Him (see Ezek. 14:22, 23; Hos. 6:1-3).

In this respect, the Old Testament is also a lesson book for the church (see 1 Cor. 10:11). Jesus wants His church to know that He is in control of the calamities and tribulations—even when His followers die as martyrs. He allows the pale rider no more territory than "a fourth of the earth" (Rev. 6:8).

In Matthew 24 Jesus described the times of religious oppression, including the final distress, as "the great tribulation" (24:21; cf. Dan. 12:1). This period would last from the destruction of Jerusalem all the way to the end of the church age. The seals portray this tribulation as religious-political warfare fought against the gospel of Jesus by riders on three horses of different colors. The colors represent the specific tasks of each rider, all of whom follow the first horse, the white horse, until the end of time.

The white horse fittingly represents the gospel rider who goes forward to conquer the hearts of men. This picture develops the previous vision in which Jesus is portrayed as the conquering Lion from the tribe of Judah (Rev. 5:5). The victorious rider on the white horse reminds us of the messianic prophecy in Psalm 45:1-5, in which the Davidic king rides forth victoriously with bow and arrows that pierce the hearts of his enemies. The following chart compares the three messianic riders on victorious battle horses:

Psalm 45:3-5 The King-Messiah	Revelation 6:2 The First Seal	Revelation 19:11, 12, 16 The Seventh Plague
"Gird your sword upon your side, O mighty one; . . . in your majesty ride forth victoriously. . . . Let your sharp arrows pierce the hearts of the king's enemies; let the nations fall beneath your feet."	Before me was a white horse! Its rider held a bow, and he was given a crown, and he rode out as a conqueror bent on conquest.	Before me was a white horse, whose rider is called Faithful and True. With justice he judges and makes war. . . . On his head are many crowns. . . . He has this name written: KING OF KINGS AND LORD OF LORDS.

The theme of the conquering Jesus runs like a thread through the Apocalypse, culminating in His triumphant return on a white horse from heaven (Rev. 19:11). The colors of the next three horses (red, black, and pale) represent the religious wars, persecutions, and executions initiated by those who oppose the gospel. These three apocalyptic riders disclose the progressive hardening of the wicked as they continue to resist the message of the white horse.

But how does God deal with the *faithful believers* who have persevered till the end during the church age? The fifth seal answers this question, describing the slain martyrs as being vindicated in heaven. There they receive "a white robe," (Rev. 6:11) because they have been faithful to "the word of God and the testimony they had maintained" (v. 9). Their spilled blood cries out incessantly to the covenant God for justice and holy revenge, just as the blood of Abel cried out to God from the ground (vs. 10, 11; Gen. 4:10).

The cry of the martyrs serves as a reminder that God will not forget His children. He does announce, however, that they will have "to wait a little longer, until the number of their fellow servants and brothers who were to be killed as they had been [is] completed" (Rev. 6:11). This indicates that a final period of distress immediately precedes the end. Daniel forecast this final tribulation (chapter 12:1), and Jesus also mentioned it (Matt. 24:21). Revelation 12–14 develops at length this final warfare against the saints. So, the fifth seal points forward to the penultimate showdown between truth and falsehood.

To comprehend the scope of the fifth seal, we need to place this seal in the perspective of Daniel's book:

Comparison of Times of Persecution

Daniel 7:25	Daniel 8:13	Daniel 12:1	Revelation 6:10, 11
"The saints will be handed over to him [the little horn] for *a time, times and*	"How long will it take for the vision to be fulfilled . . . of the host that will	*"At that time* [of the end] Michael, the great prince who protects	"How long, Sovereign Lord, . . . until you judge the inhabitants of the

Daniel 7:25	Daniel 8:13	Daniel 12:1	Revelation 6:10, 11
half a time" (emphasis added).	be trampled underfoot?"	your people, will arise [for holy war].	earth and avenge our blood?" . . .
	"It will be for a time, times and half a time" (Dan. 12:7, emphasis added).	There will be a time of distress such as has not happened from the beginning of nations until then" (emphasis added).	*They were told to wait a little longer, until the number of their fellow servants . . . to be killed . . . was completed* (emphasis added).

Daniel foretold two major periods of persecution: the three and a half "times" (Dan. 7:25; 12:7) of the "little horn" (7:8) and the final distress in "the time of the end," perpetrated by the "king of the North" (11:40-45; 12:1). The fifth seal of Revelation combines these visions of Daniel. It assures all who are faithful to the Word of God and the testimony of Jesus that divine justice will soon avenge their blood (Rev. 6:9-11).

This judgment day arrives in the sixth seal, which introduces the Judge of the earth with fearful cosmic signs (Rev. 6:12-17). Only then will the injustice of the religious-political powers be revealed. Only then will the suffering and death of the slaughtered believers be avenged. So, the seals reach their climax in the sixth seal, which describes the Day of the Lord in apocalyptic language. The message of the seals is clear: God guarantees the public vindication of the maligned saints and the punishment of all oppressive, dehumanizing powers.

Spotlight on the Last Generation

John's vision in Revelation 7 is an interlude attached to the sixth seal. It comes as a response to the desperate question of the wicked: "The great day of their wrath has come, and who can stand?" (Rev. 6:17).

Will *anybody* be able to stand in the Day of Judgment? None can stand in their own strength and moral goodness. But this vision brings the assurance that God will provide a protective shield for His faithful children! John calls this the sealing of the 144,000 true Israelites. It fulfills Jesus' promise that He will "keep" His church "from the hour of trial that is going to come upon the whole world to test those who live on the earth" (Rev. 3:10). So, Revelation 7 conveys God's assurance of eternal security to His threatened church.

This chapter's interlude consists of two parts: the vision of the 144,000 sealed Israelites (verses 1-8), and the vision of the unnumbered multitude from all nations and languages (verses 9-17). Revelation 7 corresponds to the preceding chapter by means of an inverse parallelism. The 144,000 sealed ones in chapter 7 correspond to the *living* saints of the sixth seal (Rev. 6:12-17); the great multitude in chapter 7 corresponds to all who have *died* for the sake of Jesus during the first five seals (6:1-11).

God must protect this last generation of His people if they are to stand unharmed during the outpouring of the seven last plagues. John wrote chapter 7 to show how it is possible that many *will* stand in the day of wrath. To place this important assurance in perspective, we need to relate it to two similar assurances of divine protection against God's punitive judgments—assurances that appear in the Old Testament. The first came when God brought judgment on the idolatry of Egypt. The blood of the Passover lamb applied to the doors of the Israelites' homes was God's appointed mark that they belonged to Him. God said, " 'The blood will be a sign for you on the houses where you are; *and when I see the blood, I will pass over you. No destructive plague will touch you when I strike Egypt'* " (Exod. 12:13).

No less significant is Ezekiel's vision of six angelic executioners of God's wrath in Jerusalem, after that city had refused to repent of its religious apostasy (see Ezek. 7, 8). In His mercy, God sends a special angel with a writing kit in advance of the executors. He commissions this angel, " 'Go throughout the city of Jerusalem and put a mark on the foreheads of those who grieve and lament over all the detestable things that are done in it' " (Ezek. 9:4). This merciful angel separated the repentant Israelites from those who were impenitent, apostate. He set them apart by placing a mark of acceptance on their foreheads. The sealing of the faithful remnant of Israel preceded the execution of the unrepentant.

While the primary fulfillment of this solemn vision occurred during Nebuchadnezzar's destruction of Jerusalem in 586 B.C., Revelation 7 applies it to the last generation of the Christian age:

> I saw another angel coming up from the east, having the seal of the living God. He called out in a loud voice to the four angels who had been given power to harm the land and the sea: "Do not harm the land or the sea or the trees *until we put a seal on the foreheads of the servants of our God."* Then I heard the number of those who were sealed: 144,000 from all the tribes of Israel (Rev. 7:2-4).

With this assurance of supernatural protection, Jesus demonstrates His providential care for the last generation of His people. When the final tribulation begins, only those people who do not have the seal of God on their foreheads will be harmed (see Rev. 9:4).

This apocalyptic sealing of God's people encompasses more than the inward sealing of the Holy Spirit that assures the soul of personal salvation (Eph. 1:13, 14). The apocalyptic seal protects its bearer from the wrath of God when human probation has ended. This becomes clearer when we compare the gospel seal and the end-time seal:

The gospel seal is placed:	The end-time seal is placed:
in the hearts of new believers	on foreheads of God's servants
by the Holy Spirit in the sacrament of baptism	by the holy angels during the final test of faith
to assure us that we are children of God and as an earnest of the coming inheritance (2 Cor. 1:22; Eph. 1:13, 14; 4:30).	to assure of special protection during the seven last plagues and Armageddon (Rev. 7:1-3; 9:4; 14:9-12).

One modern expositor explains the end-time focus of the 144,000 well:

The 144,000 are those Christians who are living at the time of the terrible cosmic dissolution expressing the wrath of God and of the Lamb. . . . The 144,000 are those who are alive on the "Day of the Lord" and have had no connection with idolatry or the antichrist.[3]

The second vision in Revelation 7 pictures a countless multitude from all nations and tribes, all of whom are clad in white and carry palms of victory in their hands. They all sing: " 'Salvation belongs to our God, who sits on the throne, and to the Lamb' " (Rev. 7:10). They are said to "have come out of the great tribulation" (7:14). This indicates that Revelation is portraying here all who have lived during the long centuries of the church age and have persevered till the end in their witness to the Word of God and the testimony of Jesus, despite suffering. Now they receive divine vindication. They will never again experience physical hardship, deprivation, hunger, or thirst. Jesus will wipe away all their suffering and tears. This vision of their glorification says that God has heard their cry for justice, and He has granted them complete satisfaction (7:16, 17).

The seventh seal portrays no further activity. It states only: "There was silence in heaven for about half an hour" (Rev. 8:1). The martyrs' cries for justice have been heard and acted upon. But a new series of visions will soon begin—one that will give a complementary view of the church age. Seven angels will sound seven trumpets!

The Purpose of the Seven Trumpets

The Apocalypse presents one more prophetic cycle that spans the entire Christian age: the continuous series of the trumpets and bowls (chapters 8, 9, 15, 16). In the trumpet cycle John presents a different perspective on church history than he gave in the seal cycle. While the seals inform the reader about the sufferings of faithful Christians, the trumpets deal with God's preliminary judgments on the enemies of His people.

It is essential to realize that John meant us to see these judgments as a chronological sequence. The fifth, sixth, and seventh trumpets are called "woes" (Rev. 8:13) that follow one another: "The first woe is past; two other woes are yet to come" (9:12); "the second woe has passed; the third woe is coming soon" (11:14). The third woe—the seventh trumpet—comprises the seven last plagues that fall on Babylon when the time of human probation has ended (chapters 15, 16). This arrangement of linked trumpets and plagues makes of them a chronological sequence that determines the relative time of the end in the book of Revelation. And as was true of the seals, an interlude is attached to the sixth trumpet, interrupting the series. The chapters that comprise this interlude—namely chapters 10–14, the central chapters of the Apocalypse—focus sharply on the last stage of human history.

In Revelation 8:2-6, John presents an introductory vision that shows the origin and purpose of the seven trumpets. As its main theme, this introductory vision consoles Jesus' oppressed people: It assures them that Jesus hears and responds to their prayers. We read:

Another angel, who had a golden censer, came and stood at the altar. He was given much incense to offer, with the prayers of all the saints, on the golden altar before the throne. *The smoke of the incense, together with the prayers of the saints, went up before God from the angel's hand. Then the angel took the censer, filled it with fire from the altar, and hurled it on the earth; and there came peals of thunder, rumblings, flashes of lightning and an earthquake* (Rev. 8:3-5).

This vision confirms Jesus' heavenly intercession on behalf of praying believers, including the martyrs as described in the fifth seal (Rev. 6:9-11). *The altar vision of Revelation 8, then, parallels the period of the seals in chapter 6, the time of human probation.* This vision ends with a scene that represents an act of judgment: the angel fills the censer with fire instead of incense. So, God will answer the saints' prayers by casting judgments upon earth. Then the Judge of all the earth will Himself appear amidst lightning, thunder, and a worldwide earthquake.

The trumpet blast was the standard sign of holy war in the Old Testament (Num. 10:9; Zeph. 1:16). The trumpets depict Jesus—the Lion from Judah (Rev. 5:5), or holy Warrior—sending limited judgments on the strongholds of the kingdom of darkness as warnings during the church age. He uses the traditional agents of holy war—fire, hail, the sword, plagues, darkening of the sky, even fallen angels—because all remain under His sovereign rule. The purpose of these judgments is to lead the enemies of His people to repentance.

The resemblance of the trumpets to the plagues that fell on Egypt tells us that the trumpet judgments are not simply natural disasters but God's covenant curses on the enemies of His people. The trumpets disclose the inadequacy of human kingdoms. Ultimately, the seventh trumpet declares: " 'The kingdom of the world has become the kingdom of our Lord and of his Christ, and he will reign forever and ever' " (Rev. 11:15). This outcome fulfills the promise of Daniel's scroll (see Dan. 2:44, 45; 7:27; 12:1-3).

The trumpet cycle, then, represents a sequential order of events that began in John's time and continues through the ages until the final judgment day. The seals show the sufferings of the saints. The trumpets show that God offers the wicked both mercy and time to repent. The offer is not accepted; the world will not return to God: "Nor did they repent of their murders, their magic arts, their sexual immorality or their thefts" (Rev. 9:21). But let it never be said that God has not done all in His power, even to the devastation of the earth, to bring people to their senses.

The last three trumpets—the fifth, sixth, and seventh—are characterized as three "woes" for the impenitent inhabitants of the earth (Rev. 8:13). With these end-time curses God allows an increase of darkness and demonic manifestations on the earth. So, these three trumpets are intensified judgments. They form the transition from divine warnings to the final judgments that will follow. In these woes, God permits evil to increase until it dominates the earth. In this scenario, God explicitly assures His people that no harm will come to them. They stand under His special seal of approval and protection (see Rev. 9:4). God will not allow total destruction. He limits the demonic devastation to "a third" of humankind (9:15, 18). This fraction serves to remind us that God still rules supreme.

During the period of the sixth trumpet, heaven still offers grace "from the horns of the golden altar that is before God" (Rev. 9:13). But the sixth trumpet announces that the time of human probation will end suddenly, at God's appointed hour, day, month, and year! (9:15).

Jesus' Concern for His End-time Church

Just as John attached a vision of eternal glory to the sixth seal, namely chapter 7, so he attaches to the darkness of the sixth trumpet visions that include both new commissions for the end-time church and, encouragingly, assurances of its triumph—chapters 10–14. Like the visions of chapter 7, those of these chapters transfer the reader to the time of the end, to the final events of the church age. They focus a prophetic spotlight on Jesus' pastoral concern for His flock during the end time of church history. They reveal His desire to strengthen His people with absolute confidence in preparation to witness faithfully to the Word of God and the testimony of Jesus.

A new mandate from heaven calls Jesus' followers to this task. They are to witness in spite of the fierce opposition of false prophets and threats of suffering. They will receive extraordinary power for their witness when the contest between the remnant church and the antichrist intensifies. And God will reward His witnesses with the same resurrection and ascension to heaven that Jesus Himself received:

> But after the three and a half days a breath of life from God entered them, and they stood on their feet, and terror struck those who saw them. Then they heard a loud voice from heaven saying to them, "Come up here." And they went up to heaven in a cloud, while their enemies looked on (Rev. 11:11, 12).

This is the theme of Revelation 10–14. We'll examine it in more detail in the next chapter.

---

1. See *Foxe's Book of Martyrs* (Grand Rapids, Mich.: Baker Books, 1995), 20-25.
2. *God Cares* (Nampa, Id.: Pacific Press, 1985), vol. 2:92.
3. E. Schüssler-Fiorenza, *Invitation to the Book of Revelation* (Garden City, N.Y.: Doubleday, 1981), 92.

Chapter Seven

JESUS' END-TIME MESSAGE

Revelation 10–14 contains Jesus' message for those who are His followers at the time of the end. The first two chapters of this unit, Revelation 10 and 11, introduce the end-time message.

Revelation 10 presents one of the most important visions in the Apocalypse; it describes what God does to inaugurate the time of the end. In this vision an angel opens a prophetic scroll that was sealed until the time of the sixth trumpet. Then he calls God's people to "take and eat" this opened book, which will motivate them to proclaim its end-time message (see Rev. 10:11). The solemn oath that the angel swears by the Creator of heaven and earth—that " 'there will be no more delay!' " (10:6)—reveals the seriousness of this new revelation.

The messages of Revelation 14's three angels develop more fully the brief declaration of chapter 10. This chapter is the thematic high point of John's Apocalypse. Here the gospel message is placed in its unique end-time setting, revealing how we can prepare for Jesus' second coming and how we should meet the totalitarian claims of the antichrist in the time of the end.

The end-time visions of this part of Revelation interpret the religious oppression that they describe as the outgrowth of a cosmic conflict. They present the warfare between the powers of the world and God's people as the expression of a spiritual war between God and Satan. The three angels' messages of Revelation 14 are known as the last Elijah message. Like the Old Testament prophet Elijah, Revelation 14 places before us the ultimate decision: Whom will we worship? This indeed requires our serious attention.

For the proper perspective, we need to take into view the entire range of chapters 12–14. These three chapters form a close-knit unit that shows its own forward movement from the apostolic church till the end of time. Revelation 12 briefly covers the entire history of the Christian church. Chapter 13 focuses on the two major periods of warfare against the saints. And chapter 14 concentrates exclusively on the final war against the remnant people of Jesus. The location of Jesus' warning message is instructive. It stands between the threats of the antichrist in chapter 13 and the Second Coming judgment in chapter 14:14-20.

Revelation 12 begins with two "signs in heaven": a woman clothed with the sun (v. 1) and an enormous red dragon (v. 3). The rest of chapters 12–14 describes the continuing conflict between the woman and the dragon, a conflict that threatens the faithful worshipers of God and one in which they finally are outlawed in all nations. This oppression elicits God's final wrath, expressed in the seven last plagues, against the persecutors.

God's Last Warning Message

Revelation 14 conveys God's ultimatum to a world united in rebellion against its Creator. A final manifestation of Pentecostal power will energize this proclamation of the last warning, enlightening the entire world as to the ultimate issues (Rev. 18:1). This "Elijah" appeal will ripen the world for the harvest at Jesus' second coming (14:14-20).

John introduces God's last message as follows:

"I saw another angel flying in midair, and he had the eternal gospel to proclaim to those who live on the earth—to every nation, tribe, language and people" (Rev. 14:6).

The message of the first angel of Revelation 14 essentially corresponds to that of the mighty angel of chapter 10, as can be seen in this comparison:

Revelation 10:5, 6	Revelation 14:6, 7
The angel I had seen standing on the sea and on the land raised his right hand to heaven. And he swore by him who lives forever and ever, who created the heavens . . . , the earth . . . , and the sea . . . , and said, *"There will be no more delay!"* (emphasis added).	I saw another angel flying in midair, and he had the eternal gospel to proclaim to those who live on the earth. . . . He said in a loud voice, "Fear God and give him glory, *because the hour of his judgment has come.* Worship him who made the heavens, the earth, the sea and the springs of water" (emphasis added).

This comparison shows that the angel of Revelation 14 places the same emphasis on worshiping *the Creator* as the angel of chapter 10 stressed in his oath. Both angels also announce with urgency that the final stage of history has begun. When their messages go forth, the world has apparently apostatized from recognizing the Creator of heaven and earth.

This description fits our time! Since Darwin's epoch-making book *The Origin of Species* was published in 1859, the world has increasingly fallen under the spell of the theory of evolution. This philosophical hypothesis considers the Bible's Creation narratives an unbelievable myth. In doing so, it denies the existence of a Creator who made us in His own image, and it leaves the universe without moral purpose or meaning—even declaring that the cosmos will eventually burn out into nothingness. So, the end-time appeal of John's Apocalypse that we worship the Creator speaks to the key philosophy of our time! On the one hand, the rejection of the Genesis account challenges the existence of a moral God and of His plan of salvation. On the other, the great truth of Creation stands as the foundation on which the whole structure of Bible doctrine is reared.

During the sixth trumpet, the angel announces that the seventh trumpet will soon sound and that God will then complete His purpose for the world (Rev. 10:7). The seventh trumpet will terminate the mystery of God. Revelation 10 thus points the reader *to the last stage of the history of salvation, the one immediately preceding the seventh trumpet!*

The angel of chapter 10 brought an unsealed scroll from heaven that lay open in his hand, announcing that the predicted "mystery of God" will be accomplished *without further delay, before the seventh angel sounds his trumpet* (see Rev. 10:6, 7). This "mystery of God" has deep Old Testament roots. It denotes God's mysterious will for the future, as Daniel explained to the king of Babylon: " 'There is a God in heaven who reveals *mysteries.* He has shown King Nebuchadnezzar *what will happen in days to come' "* (Dan. 2:28). The apostle Paul explained that his gospel proclamation of Christ Jesus was "the *mystery* hidden for long ages past, but now revealed and made known . . . so that all nations might believe and obey him" (Rom. 16:25, 26; see also Eph. 3:2-6). Jesus declared, " 'This gospel of the kingdom will be preached in the whole world as a testimony to all nations, *and then the end will come' "* (Matt. 24:14).

The revival of the apostolic gospel is central to God's plan and to His end-time work. Mark 13:10 says, " 'The gospel must *first* be preached to all nations.' " To proclaim the gospel in its end-time setting of Revelation 12–14 is the church's final mission. The worldwide gospel proclamation demonstrates the presence of the last Elijah. The fulfilling of this mission is the greatest sign of all that the time of the end has begun!

Revelation 14:6's phrase "the eternal gospel" carries special meaning. It stresses that the end-time gospel proclamation is the same gospel the apostles of Jesus preached and wrote down in Scripture. Not even an angel has the authority to change the gospel of God's free and sovereign grace (see Gal. 1:6-9). This "everlasting gospel" becomes extremely relevant when viewed in its end-time setting of Revelation 13, which says the antichrist will demand allegiance to his counterfeit gospel (v. 5; cf. 2 Cor. 11:4).

Both chapters 10 and 14 direct their final warning to the whole world. The angel that flies "in midair" in Revelation 14 intends a worldwide extension of his message, just as the mighty angel of Revelation 10 plants his feet on both sea and land. This universal scope is emphasized in the fourfold phrase: "to every nation, tribe, language and people" (Rev. 14:6). So, Revelation 14 predicts a *worldwide revival of the apostolic gospel* as the message that prepares people for the end. Revelation 10 and 14, then, is the end-time fulfillment of Jesus' prediction in Matthew 24:14.

While the angel of Revelation 10 indicates the end-time *setting* of this warning message, the angels of Revelation 14 develop the *content* of the message itself. Now chapter 10's scroll is unrolled, revealing a threefold message that applies to the time immediately preceding Jesus' second coming (Rev. 14:14-20).

The Restoration of the Eternal Gospel

A better understanding of the gospel creates a new people. God commissions them as ambassadors to proclaim the gospel in its apocalyptic setting of Revelation 12–14. The angel of Revelation 14 called the message he delivered the "eternal gospel" to identify it, because there will be a universal apostasy from the apostolic gospel in the time of the end. This brings us to a brief consideration of the content of the gospel.

Paul explained the gospel with apostolic authority and clarity in Romans 1–8. He wrote a summary of it in 1 Corinthians 15: "I received . . . as of first importance: that Christ died for our sins according to the Scriptures, that he was buried, [and] that he was raised on the third day according to the Scriptures" (verses 3, 4). This makes the proclamation of the atoning death of Jesus, the foundation of the doctrine of justification by faith, a touchstone of faithfulness to the Word of God. *Apostasy from this gospel is no less serious than apostasy from the law of God.* This was Martin Luther's great discovery in the sixteenth century. Luther was the "Elijah" of his time in Europe—a true forerunner of the worldwide reformation in the time of the end.

The first angel's message is extremely relevant for our day because many now deny the Pauline doctrine of justification by faith in Jesus. Or they accept compromising definitions for the purpose of establishing a formal unity of Christendom.

The angel makes an urgent appeal to all who live on earth: " 'Worship him who made the heavens, the earth, the sea and the springs of water' " (Rev. 14:7). This call for true worship is borrowed from the Old Testament; it repeats the claim of Israel's God for exclusive rights to worship because He created heaven and earth.

Heaven's call has practical implications. Israel worshiped God for two specific reasons: because He is the Creator of all reality and because He is also the Redeemer of His creation. The following two passages spell out these reasons:

> Remember the Sabbath day by keeping it holy. . . . For in six days the LORD made the heavens and the earth, the sea, and all that is in them, but he rested on the seventh day. Therefore the LORD blessed the Sabbath day and made it holy (Exod. 20:8, 11).
>
> Remember that you were slaves in Egypt and that the LORD your God brought you out of there with a mighty hand and an outstretched arm. *Therefore* the LORD your God has commanded you to observe the Sabbath day (Deut. 5:15).

Israel's celebration of the seventh-day Sabbath set her apart from all Gentile nations. Her worship identified the God of Israel, YAHWEH, as the Creator of heaven and earth and as the Redeemer of His covenant people. People often overlook the fact that the Sabbath day was also the appointed sign of Israel's deliverance from Egypt, as Moses explained. This should be no surprise, because Israel's Redeemer claimed to be the Creator of heaven and earth (Exod. 20:11). True

Sabbath keeping thus honors God as both Creator and Redeemer.

Jesus called Himself " 'the Lord of the Sabbath' " (Matt. 12:8), which implies the claim that He was the Creator of the Sabbath and the Provider of Sabbath rest for all people. As the true Interpreter of the Sabbath commandment, He kept that day in the Spirit and in truth (Luke 4:16; John 15:10). And He offers Sabbath rest to all who come to Him (see Matt. 11:28, 29). Christian Sabbath keeping recognizes Jesus as the Lord of the Sabbath and of all creation. In Jesus the seventh-day Sabbath functions as the sacrament of the rest of His redeeming grace, which is available every day (see Heb. 4:9-11, 16).

The first angel of Revelation 14 makes worshiping the Creator a testing truth, a test of loyalty to the gospel. His appeal intends to restore true worship and communion with God, as taught by Jesus and His apostles. The remnant church will once again stand in the true line of apostolic succession.

We need to give special attention to the new motivation for worshiping the Creator: " 'because the hour of his judgment has come!' " (Rev. 14:7). The claim that God is the Judge of all peoples since He has created all people appears frequently in the Old Testament (Gen. 18:25; Ps. 96:5, 10, 13). Jesus and the apostles repeated this message, especially in light of Jesus' messiahship and His claim that God " 'has given him authority to judge because he is the Son of Man' " (John 5:27; see also 12:48; Dan. 7:13, 14). Paul made the coming judgment an integral part of his gospel message (Rom. 2:5-13). He declared to governor Felix that he should reckon with "the judgment to come" (Acts 24:25). But the angel of Revelation 14 adds a new urgency: the hour of God's judgment *has come!* This announcement takes on special meaning in view of the antichrist's worldwide misuse of judicial systems to persecute the saints, as described in Revelation 13:15-17.

In what sense is it true that the hour of God's judgment *has come?* This may be understood in two complementary respects. First, we should relate it to God's executive judgment that comes with the Second Coming, as portrayed vividly in the vision of Revelation 14:14-20. In this respect, the phrase "has come" functions as a proleptic or "prophetic perfect," in which the past tense is used to describe a future event. Israel's prophets frequently used the prophetic perfect to emphasize the certainty of the fulfillment of their predictions (see Isa. 53; 63; Jude 14, 15, RSV, NASB). John also used the prophetic perfect (see Rev. 13:4). The first angel, then, announces *the judgment that approaches in Jesus' second coming.*

There is, however, another dimension that is commonly neglected and comes to light only when the phrase is placed in the larger perspective of the book of Daniel. The setting of Daniel 7 is that of judgment in a chronological framework that no other book of the Old Testament presents. Here we discover a new aspect of Revelation 14's warning that the hour of God's judgment *has* come. We need to consider the central judgment vision of Daniel (7:9, 10).

The Timing of God's Judgment

"As I looked, thrones were set in place, and the Ancient of Days took his seat. His clothing was as white as snow; the hair of his head was white like wool. His throne was flaming with fire, and its wheels were all ablaze. A river of fire was flowing, coming out from before him. Thousands upon thousands attended him; ten thousand times ten thousand stood before him. *The court was seated, and the books were opened"* (Daniel 7:9, 10).

The immediate context reveals the purpose of this end-time judgment in the heavenly throne room. This scene is meant to show God's judgment of the powers persecuting His saints. He will reverse the travesties of justice perpetrated against them, restore the dignity of His faithful ones, and reward them with a glorious resurrection and reign on earth.

Daniel provides an inspired interpretation of his judgment vision:

"As I watched, this horn was waging war against the saints and defeating them, *until the Ancient of Days came and pronounced judgment in favor of the saints of the Most High, and the time came when they possessed the kingdom"* (Dan. 7:22).

The context of Daniel 7 teaches that the heavenly court pronounces verdicts concerning *both* the persecuting horn and the persecuted saints. But these verdicts differ. While the persecuting powers are justly condemned, the maligned saints are vindicated (Dan. 7:22). God's judgment, then, will separate the true Israel of God from the wicked. Daniel 12:1-3, which parallels this portion of chapter 7, provides an important supplement to this judgment scene:

> "At that time [of the end] your people—everyone whose name is found written in the book—will be delivered. Multitudes who sleep in the dust of the earth will awake: some to everlasting life, others to shame and everlasting contempt."

Here the righteous and the wicked *within* Israel are separated, and only those who are inscribed in the "book" are delivered. In other words, the "book" determines who is worthy of resurrection and eternal life in God's kingdom. This is the reassuring news of Daniel's investigative judgment, which takes place in heaven *before* Jesus' second advent.

The timing Daniel's vision sets for the heavenly court session is instructive. The judgment begins *after* the wicked horn has persecuted the saints for three and a half prophetic "times" (Dan. 7:25). The start of the heavenly court session coincides with its proclamation on earth, when the angel of Revelation 14 begins to warn the world that the hour of God's judgment has come. We can visualize this synchronizing of Daniel 7 and Revelation 14 in the following diagram:

Daniel 7:9-11	Revelation 14:6, 7
"As I looked [while the little horn "spoke boastfully"], *thrones were set in place, and the Ancient of Days took his seat. . . . The court was seated, and the books were opened.* Then I continued to watch because of the boastful words the horn was speaking" (emphasis added).	I saw another angel flying in midair [in the end-time]. . . . He said in a loud voice, *"Fear God and give him glory, because the hour of his judgment has come. Worship him who made the heavens, the earth, the sea and the springs of wate*r" (emphasis added).

The vision of Daniel 7 and the message of the first angel of Revelation 14 both focus on the time of the end. The beginning of the judgment in heaven, predicted in Daniel 7, and the beginning of the proclamation of the three messengers of Revelation 14 coincide.

Connecting the first angel's message with Daniel 7 sheds new light on the meaning of the announcement "the hour of God's judgment has come." It indicates that the angel is announcing that the *pre-Advent* judgment in heaven has begun! This proclamation on earth coincides with the beginning of the final phase of God's work for our salvation in heaven.

Daniel's angel commanded that he "close up and seal the words of the scroll until the time of the end. Many will go here and there to increase knowledge" (Dan. 12:4). In other words, Daniel's end-time visions were not relevant for God's people *until* the time of the end had arrived. The beginning of that epoch is revealed only when one sees the parallel structure of Daniel 7 and 8. The vision of Daniel 8 complements Daniel 7 with a promise that God's sanctuary will be restored to its rightful function at "the appointed time of the end"—that is, when the 2,300 "days" have expired (8:14, 19)! Students of prophecy in both Europe and America discovered this truth about God's sanctuary in the nineteenth century. Their discovery empowered the great second-advent awakening in the Christian world.[1]

The Second Angel's Message

The second angel of Revelation 14 announces " 'Fallen! Fallen is Babylon the Great,' " because she " 'made all the nations drink the maddening wine of her adulteries' " (Rev. 14:8). To understand the symbolic meaning of "Babylon the Great," we must ask the biblical text for clarification. Again, the Old Testament provides the key that unlocks the mystery. "Babylon the Great" was Israel's archenemy in Daniel's time (see Dan. 4:30). That nation invaded Israel's land, destroyed Solomon's temple with its atoning services, and carried God's covenant people away as captives (see Dan. 1:1, 2).

In the book of Revelation, then, "Babylon" signifies the archenemy of the new-covenant people, Jesus' church. (The existence of a spiritual Babylon presupposes the existence of a spiritual Israel, the people of God. These end-time people qualify as saints because they have responded to the first angel's message.) Just as ancient Babylon was declared guilty in God's judgment and then suffered the destruction of its kingdom (Dan. 5:27), so God announces that end-time Babylon has also "fallen" and will soon be destroyed. This typological connection of the two Babylons is the key to under-standing the second angel's message.

We're not left to speculate as to who Babylon is. An angel explains it, using the symbol of a fallen woman who brazenly seeks an illicit love-relation with the kings of the earth instead of with her husband Jesus. The result is appalling:

"I saw that the woman was drunk with the blood of the saints, the blood of those who bore testimony to Jesus. When I saw her, I was greatly astonished" (Rev. 17:6).

John expected persecution from the Roman Empire since he had already experienced it personally (see Rev. 1:9). But this revelation that the *institutional church* would use the strong arm of the State to shed the blood of the followers of Jesus shocked him.

John distinguishes clearly between the apostate *religious body* (the fallen woman) and *political powers* (the kings of the earth) in his vision of Revelation 17. He says the inhabitants of the earth will all be affected because they will be "intoxicated with the wine of her adulteries" (Rev. 17:2). His words picture worldwide deception and a universal alliance against the people of Jesus. The prostitute's "fornication" with the worldly powers represents the unlawful union of the Christian church with the political powers of the earth, which began when Emperor Constantine created the state-church in the fourth century and con-tinued when the popes created the persecuting church-state with its episcopal and papal inquisitions in the Middle Ages.[2]

The wine that intoxicates the nations of the earth apparently rep-resents the false doctrines that corrupt the truths of the Bible. Among them are the perversion of the saving gospel by a doctrine of meritorious works, sacraments, and priesthood; the ritual of infant baptism that has turned a church of believers into a worldly church; the unauthorized change of the seventh-day Sabbath of the commandment into the Sunday-Sabbath; and the doctrine of the natural immortality of the soul—adopted from pagan mythology—that gives people false hopes and opens the door to spiritism. The entire world has become drunk with the wine of Babylon so that it does not distinguish anymore between the holy and the unholy, between the Creator and the creation, between God's Word and the word of church traditions and human philosophies.

Heaven's proclamation "Babylon has fallen" is God's judicial verdict on the unfaithful Christian church. Daniel recorded the verdict published by the mysterious handwriting on the wall of ancient Babylon: " 'You have been weighed on the scales and found wanting' " (Dan. 5:27). The destruction of that Babylon followed soon afterwards (5:30). So it will be again in the case of end-time Babylon: the third angel warns of the execution of the verdict—the outpouring of the pure wrath of God (Rev. 14:9-11). The three angels of Revelation 14, then, urge all the saints to leave Babylon, just as Jesus counseled His followers to flee from Jerusalem because of her impending doom (Matt. 24:15-20).

Revelation 18 makes explicit for the last generation this end-time call to leave the unfaithful Christian churches:

"Come out of her, my people, so that you will not share in her sins, so that you will not receive any of her plagues; for her sins are piled up to heaven, and God has remembered her crimes" (Rev. 18:4, 5).

Revelation 18 forecasts the rise of a movement within Christianity that will call for reformation of worship at a time when the apostolic gospel is revived with Pentecostal power (see 18:1-5). The announcement of the impending "plagues" (18:4) means that there's still time for people to leave Babylon, which only the last plagues will destroy (16:17-19). Clearly, the messages of Revelation 14 convey the final warning to a world united in rebellion against the Creator-Redeemer and His people. God's grace finally reaches its limits when Babylon's crimes "are piled up to heaven."

The three angels draw a clear line of demarcation between Babylon and the Israel of God. They identify the ultimate standard of truth as the "eternal gospel," which they also define as the commandments of God and the faith of Jesus (Rev. 14:6, 12). This prophetic message becomes *present truth* in the time of the end!

The Third Angel's Message

The third angel addresses his warning to every person on earth: " 'If anyone worships the beast and his image and receives his mark on the forehead or on the hand, he, too will drink of the wine of God's fury, which has been poured full strength into the cup of his wrath' " (Rev. 14:9, 10). This dreadful pronouncement warns of the consequences of accepting Babylon's intoxicating wine (14:8): All who drink it must *also* drink the cup of God's wrath! (John has borrowed this imagery directly from the judgment oracles of Israel's prophets [see Isa. 51:17, 22; Jer. 25:15, 16, 27; Ezek. 23:31-34].) The impenitent worshipers of the antichrist-beast must drink God's wrath "in full strength"—that is, no longer mixed with divine mercy. This wrath of God is poured out as the seven last plagues (Rev. 15:1). The third angel thus warns against God's retributive judgment—the bowl plagues that culminate in Armageddon (16:13-16).

Both Jesus and the antichrist require the undivided allegiance of their worshipers, the complete devotion of their thinking and acting ("forehead" and "hand"). The rival systems of worship differ in that the beast uses deceptive miracles and political coercion to win adherents (16:13, 14; 19:20), while the Lamb of God uses spiritual persuasion through His Word and His Spirit. Those who remain faithful to authentic worship have learned to distrust the modern wonders and miracles that so easily deceive human beings (see Rev. 13:14; 19:20; Matt. 24:24). Instead, they trust only the "word of God and the testimony of Jesus" (Rev. 1:9; 6:9; 12:17; 14:12; 20:4).

The three angels of Revelation 14 function as the last Elijah in salvation history. God sends them forth in a time of global apostasy with a message to restore Jesus' ministry in our worship. Just as the first Elijah placed before Israel the ultimate decision of faith—whom to worship and to follow (see 1 Kings 18:21)—so the last Elijah brings to all people the hour of decision regarding the authority of Scripture and whom to worship. The angel calls for a wholehearted return to our Creator and Redeemer. This is the essence of true revival and reformation!

We must face some of the modern Baals:

> In the exaltation of the human above the divine, in the praise of popular leaders, in the worship of mammon, and in the placing of the teachings of science above the truths of revelation, multitudes today are following after Baal.[3]

Our response to heaven's final appeal will determine our eternal destiny. The first Elijah received a marvelous reward when he completed his mission: "Suddenly a chariot of fire and horses of fire appeared . . . and Elijah went up to heaven in a whirlwind" (2 Kings 2:11). Elijah didn't die. He was translated into glory!

This is the reassuring promise for the final generation of Jesus' witnesses. When Jesus, appearing in all His glory, descends through the eastern skies on His white horse, myriads of angels will accompany Him "riding on white horses" (Rev. 19:11, 14). They come to deliver the saints from their oppressors and to lift them into the presence of the King of kings. Revelation 19:19-21 describes the alternative: the destiny of the beast, his false prophet, and all their followers.

The decrees of heaven make this outcome certain (Rev. 22:11). Our challenge is to understand God's end-time message and to make the right decision of faith—that of worshiping God according to His will.

---

1. See L. E. Froom, *The Prophetic Faith of Our Fathers* (Hagerstown, Md.: Review & Herald, 1954), vol. 4; W. L. Emmerson, *The Reformation and the Advent Movement* (Hagerstown, Md.: Review & Herald, 1983).
2. See H. C. Lea, *The Inquisition of the Middle Ages* (New York: Barnes & Noble, 1993).
3. Ellen G. White, *Prophets and Kings* (Hagerstown, Md.: Review & Herald, 1943), 170.

Chapter Eight

THE MEANING
OF
ARMAGEDDON

To understand Armageddon, we must allow the Bible to interpret itself. The result will surprise those who accept the popular concepts of this subject that many Christian books and magazines foist upon their readers.

The term *Armageddon* occurs only once in the entire Bible, in Revelation 16:16: "They [the "spirits of demons performing miraculous signs," v. 14] gathered the kings together to the place that in Hebrew is called Armageddon." Because the Bible uses this term only once, we're entirely dependent on the context for its meaning.

Armageddon appears as the climax of Revelation 16's seven last plagues. These plagues express the "wrath of God" against a world united in rebellion against its Creator and His worshipers (Rev. 15:1; 18:4-6). Surprisingly, three *religious* powers, portrayed as "the dragon, the beast, and the false prophet" (Rev. 16:13), will spearhead this uprising against God. The persecuting power of these religious institutions comes from their union with political powers (16:14). Their participation makes the war of Armageddon in essence a religious-political war against the true worshipers of God.

Revelation's explanation of Armageddon vividly portrays the purpose of the final unification of all religious and political powers:

> "They will make war against the Lamb, but the Lamb will overcome them because he is Lord of lords and King of kings—and with him will be his called, chosen, and faithful followers." . . . Then I saw the beast and the kings of the earth and their armies gathered together to make war against the rider on the horse and his army [the Lamb and His followers]. But the beast was captured, and with him the false prophet who had performed the miraculous signs on his behalf (Rev. 17:14; 19:19, 20).

This is the biblical portrayal of Armageddon. That battle is not some nuclear accident that destroys the world. Nor is it World War III. In the Armageddon the Bible portrays, God is the protagonist and His people are at the heart of the final conflict!

God's War Against His Enemies

Armageddon is the grand finale of all God's holy wars. To understand this battle, we need to recognize the correspondence between God's past acts of rescue and this one of the future.

In the battle of Armageddon, God Himself acts on behalf of His people just as He did when Israel cried out to Him for help while they suffered in Egypt. Of that experience Moses explained, "God heard their groaning and he remembered his covenant with Abraham, with Isaac and with Jacob" (Exod. 2:24). Faithful to His promises, God poured out ten plagues on the oppressors. He turned the water of the Nile into blood, sent devastating frogs, flies, gnats, locusts, hail, festering boils, total darkness, and finally the sudden death of the firstborn of every Egyptian (Exod. 7–12). The message was repeated: " 'Then you will know that the LORD makes a distinction between Egypt and Israel' " (Exod. 11:7). God brought " 'judgment on all the gods of Egypt' " while protecting Israel from every " 'destructive plague' " (Exod. 12:12, 13).

When, in their escape from Egypt, the Israelites were about to cross the Red Sea, Pharaoh pursued them with his army. But Moses encouraged the frightened Israelites: " 'Do not be afraid. Stand firm and you will see the deliverance the LORD will bring you today. The Egyptians you see today you will never see again. *The Lord will fight for you; you need only to be still*' " (Exod. 14:13, 14). This historic deliverance of Israel was a holy war in which God manifested His covenant faithfulness.

After their miraculous rescue, Moses and the Israelites sang a victory song known as the "song of Moses" (see Rev. 15:3). With poetic fervor, Moses praised Yahweh as the "warrior" King who had redeemed them from their persecutors:

"The LORD, the Warrior—LORD is His name! Pharaoh's chariots and his army He has cast into the sea; . . . Your right hand, O LORD, glorious in power, Your right hand, O LORD, shatters the foe! . . . Who is like You, O LORD, among the celestials; Who is like You, majestic in holiness, Awesome in splendor, working wonders!" (Exod. 15:3, 5, 11, The New Jewish Publication Society Translation, 1992).

The book of Revelation refers to the song of Moses as a prophetic type of the deliverance of Christ's people at the end of time. The last generation of saints will join Israel in singing "the song of Moses the servant of God and the song of the Lamb" (Rev. 15:3). The theme of dramatic rescue will be the same: " 'Great and marvelous are your deeds, Lord God Almighty. Just and true are your ways, King of the ages . . . *for your righteous acts have been revealed*' " (15:3, 4). The followers of Jesus sing this song after the battle of Armageddon liberates them from Babylon.

The Destruction of End-time Babylon

One of the seven angels who delivered the plagues led John to understand that Babylon fell primarily because of her bloodthirsty persecution of the Christian witnesses. John wrote, "I saw that the woman [Babylon] was drunk with the blood of the saints, the blood of those who bore testimony to Jesus" (Rev. 17:6). This attitude of cruel intolerance for those who bore witness about Jesus and His gospel characterizes end-time Babylon. It causes the Defender of the true witnesses to bring about her doom. Babylon's destruction comes as the seventh plague: "God remembered Babylon the Great and gave her the cup filled with the wine of the fury of his wrath" (16:19). Armageddon also takes place during the seventh plague. Therefore, Armageddon *is* the destruction of worldwide Babylon.

The bowl plagues of Revelation 16 are not arbitrary outbursts of a capricious or vindictive God. Revelation portrays them as the global antitype of the ten plagues on Egypt. And they have the same purpose: to redeem God's beleaguered people and to manifest the righteousness of the covenant God to the oppressors of His people.

God's love moves Him to send a timely warning to all nations about the danger of conforming to the will of the beast by "drinking the wine of the wrath" of Babylon:

"If anyone worships the beast and its image, and receives a mark on his forehead or on his hand, he also shall drink the wine of God's wrath, poured *unmixed* into the cup of his anger, and he shall be tormented with fire and sulphur in the presence of the holy angels and in the presence of the Lamb" (Rev. 14:9, 10, RSV).

This warning from heaven announces God's "wrath," or retributive righteousness, unmixed with divine mercy. God cannot be mocked. No one needs to side with Babylon by accepting the "mark of the beast." No one needs to be lost! Everyone is invited to receive the "seal of the living God" and to take his or her stand with the faithful remnant of worshipers of the Creator. Jesus assured: " 'Whoever acknowledges me before men, I will also acknowledge him before my Father in heaven' " (Matt. 10:32).

God does not pour out His wrath indiscriminately on the last generation the way an earthquake kills all people without distinction.

The plagues are directed exclusively to those who have accepted "the mark of the beast" (Rev. 16:2, 10, 11). They target Babylon alone, because "her sins are piled up to heaven, and God has remembered her crimes" against His people and against humanity (18:4, 5, 20). An angel explains: " 'In her was found the blood of the prophets and of the saints, and of all who have been killed on the earth' " (18:24). After Babylon's judgment, the heavenly beings gratefully sing " 'Hallelujah! Salvation and glory and power belong to our God, for true and just are his judgments. He has condemned the great prostitute who corrupted the earth by her adulteries. *He has avenged on her the blood of his servants'* " (19:1, 2).

So, the book of Revelation constitutes the counterpart of the four Gospels, which focus on God's mercy to repentant sinners. God's character is determined by His *holy* love, and His holy love encompasses both atonement for sin and the ultimate removal of sin. The "wrath of God" does not express God's eternal character but His historical reaction to sin: His judgment, or condemnation, of evil. The counterpart of this wrath is God's gift of eternal life, or salvation (see Rom. 2:5-11).

The divine infliction of wrath belongs to God's faithfulness and justice (Rom. 3:3-6). As one scholar explained, "God continues to be the Judge, and Christian faith in the grace of God does not consist in the conviction that God's wrath does not exist or that there is no threateningly impending judgment (2 Cor. 5:10), but in the conviction of being rescued from God's wrath."[1] This rescue depends completely on whether a person rejects Jesus or appropriates Him and His gospel. John summed it all up in these words: "He who has the Son has life; he who does not have the Son of God does not have life" (1 John 5:12).

The three angels of Revelation 14 announce the coming of the "unmixed" wrath of God, which consists of the plagues that culminate in Armageddon (Rev. 15:1; 16:13-16). This places a special responsibility on those who proclaim the last warning message of God: They must teach the biblical meaning of Armageddon as part of the three angels' messages. They are not called to be prophets themselves or to speculate about a third world war, but to engage in a responsible exegesis of Scripture that respects the biblical context of Armageddon and focuses on its Christ-centered test of faith.

The Sola Scriptura Principle

To avoid misinterpreting the Bible, one must recognize the organic nature of Holy Scripture; that is, the spiritual unity of divine revelation. No part may be dissected from the totality and given some sensational application to fit modern events. The temptation to read present-day newspaper reports directly into biblical prophecy continually lurks near. While history is the ultimate confirmation of divine prediction, we must never take the shifting sands of secular events as the guiding norm for interpreting Bible prophecies. We must be committed to the basic axiom of faith that *the Bible is its own interpreter*.

The Protestant Reformation of the sixteenth century posited belief in the *sola Scriptura* principle in opposition to the Roman Catholic belief that the teaching "magisterium" (that is, the pope and his bishops) has the sole authority for determining the meaning of Scripture. Protestant faith affirms a personal responsibility for searching the Scriptures to find the message God intended them to convey. The apostle Paul himself submitted to the scrutiny of the Jews in Berea when he expounded the gospel of Jesus Christ. "Now the Bereans were of more noble character than the Thessalonians," Luke wrote, "for they received the message with great eagerness *and examined the Scriptures every day to see if what Paul said was true*" (Acts 17:11). Divine truth was not determined simply by Paul's claim to be an apostle of God, but by the essential harmony of his message with the Hebrew canon of Scripture.

The ancient norm of truth—"To the law and to the testimony! If they do not speak according to this word, they have no light of dawn" (Isa. 8:20)—remains relevant for Christians. Jesus confirmed this criterion when He stated, " 'They have Moses and the Prophets; let them listen to them' " (Luke 16:29). Because Jesus spoke only what God wanted Him to speak, He could say: " 'There is a judge for the one who rejects me and does not accept my words; *that very word which I spoke will condemn him at the last day' "* (John 12:48). Jesus' teachings carry the same authority as the words of the Hebrew prophets; they constitute God's final and definitive revelation to mankind (see Heb. 1:1, 2; 10:28-31).

All this means that our interpretation of Armageddon, the apocalyptic war, must harmonize with the past revelations about God's holy wars. John's Apocalypse does not suddenly reveal a climax of salvation history that differs essentially from that portrayed by Israel's prophets. The New Testament does not abolish the Old Testament scenario of the end; it advances and develops it in a glorious Christocentric consummation. This unfolding revelation confirms the essential harmony of the Old and New Testament perspectives on the end.

This understanding leads to another principle of prophetic interpretation: We must view the war of Armageddon in terms of *its progressive clarification in the book of Revelation*. The context, in particular Revelation 17:12-16; 19:11-21, enlightens us regarding the meaning of Armageddon.

These two aids to the biblical understanding of Armageddon—the wider Hebrew context and the immediate context in the Apocalypse—complement each other and safeguard the theological unity of biblical eschatology. Scripture's portrayal of Babylon's war against God and the Lamb does not support any of the Middle East speculations so dominant in the popular presentations of today. This leads us to an examination of the New Testament application of the territorial promises made to Israel.

Jesus' Teaching Regarding the Holy Land

The New Testament unanimously declares all the old covenant's ethnic and geographic restrictions removed. Theologically speaking, Jesus' twelve apostles are the continuation of the twelve tribes of Israel. And the New Testament addresses the apostolic church as the *new Israel* (see James 1:1; 1 Pet. 1:1; Gal. 3:29; 6:16) and says it has inherited ancient Israel's calling to be "a light for the

Gentiles" (Exod. 19:5, 6; Isa. 42:6, 7; 1 Pet. 2:9, 10; Matt. 5:14). The new-covenant people are no longer delimited by race or territory, but solely by faith in Jesus as the Christ, the Messiah of Israel (see Rom. 10:9-13). Nowhere does the New Testament envision a political reconstitution of Israel as a nation or national theocracy.[2] The Incarnation marks a radically new beginning of salvation history.

When, in Old Testament times, God promised Israel a land in which they could dwell in safety, He was speaking of Palestine. Jesus applied that promise to the earth made new: "Blessed are the meek, for *they will inherit the earth*" (Matt. 5:5)! This "land" will be infinitely larger than what David envisioned (Ps. 37:11); the ultimate fulfillment will include the entire earth in its recreated beauty (see Isa. 11:6-9; Rev. 21, 22). The renewed earth will be the inheritance of the meek from all nations who accept Jesus as their Lord and Savior. Jesus did not spiritualize away Israel's territorial promise. Rather, He widened the scope till it extended to the whole world. This is the principle of *universalizing the land promises.*

The classic passage in which Jesus taught the universal enlargement of Israel's holy territory is His revelation to the Samaritan woman. She asked which mountain was the true holy place where people should worship God, Mount Gerizim in Samaria or Mount Zion in Jerusalem. Jesus replied, " 'Believe me, woman, a time is coming when you will worship the Father *neither on this mountain nor in Jerusalem*' " (John 4:21). With these words Jesus abolished all holy places on earth, proclaiming instead that *He* as the Messiah is now the appointed "holy place": " 'One greater than the temple is here' " (Matt. 12:6)! So both Israel and the Gentiles must gather to Him. He invites, " *'Come to me,* all you who are weary and burdened, and I will give you rest' " (Matt. 11:28; cp. 23:37).

The underlying principle is clear. Wherever Jesus is, that is the holy place! Jesus affirmed this when He claimed: " 'Where two or three come together in my name, there am I with them' " (Matt. 18:20). In place of the old temple's Shekinah holiness the New Testament substitutes the holiness of the Lord Jesus. Those who come to Jesus have come to Mount Zion, the temple mountain, the place of God's presence (see Heb. 12:22-24; Rev. 14:1). This truth is an essential part of the apostolic gospel.

Jesus did not present one eschatological hope for Jewish Christians and an entirely different one for Gentile Christians. He announced that believers in His Messiahship will be brought together from all nations into "one flock" under "one shepherd" (John 10:16). One radical principle guided Jesus' applications of the promises made to Israel: the removal of all ethnic and geographic restrictions for the new-covenant people. The reason is simple: God's promise to Abraham that he would become the father of "many nations" (Gen. 17:5) will be fulfilled through Jesus! Paul explained: "Therefore, the promise comes by faith, so that it may be by grace and may be guaranteed to all Abraham's offspring—not only to those who are of the law but also to those who are of the faith of Abraham. He is the father of us all" (Rom. 4:16). Here Paul rejects the hermeneutic of literalism by his theological exegesis of Genesis 17:5. "Paul understood that Abraham would father a multitude of nations through Christ."[3]

The land that God promised to Abraham and his seed was a type of the world (see Rom. 4:13). The full scope of the prophecies regarding Israel was not nationalistic but universal and even included the surprising dimensions of "a new heaven and a new earth" (2 Pet. 3:13; see also Isa. 65:17). The guiding principle for the Christian understanding of the Old Testament is this: We must understand it the way Jesus and the New Testament understand it. The Old Testament no longer has the last word! Jesus and the New Testament have the final authority about the fulfillment of the Old Testament. Such is the transforming power of the gospel of Jesus.

Old Testament Types Foreshadow Armageddon

The symbolic name *Armageddon* can be translated as either "Mountain of Slaughter" or "Mountain of Megiddo." So, Revelation 16's battle of Armageddon reminds us of Israel's holy war against Sisera, the commander of the Canaanite kings, near "the waters of Megiddo" (Judges 5:19). When Sisera with his nine hundred iron chariots attacked Israel, "the stars" from heaven fought together with Israel by sending a sudden rainfall that bogged down the hostile chariots (5:20). Thus the God of Israel went out before His people and routed Sisera (4:14, 15). This victory was of such historic importance that Israel memorialized it in the Song of Deborah (5:10, 11).

Another significant conflict occurred near Megiddo, this one involving worship. In this showdown between the prophet Elijah and the prophets of Baal, fire came down from heaven to prove that Yahweh, Israel's God, was the true God (see 1 Kings 18:19-40). The confrontation ended with the execution of the false prophets. The symbolic portrayal of the opposing forces at Armageddon —"the dragon, the beast, and the false prophet" versus Jesus and His chosen people—reminds us of that historic clash. Jon Paulien keenly notes: "If John was alluding to Elijah's experience on Mount Carmel, he understood the battle of Armageddon to be a spiritual conflict over worship (cp. Rev. 13:4, 8, 12, 15; 14:7, 9, 11; cp. 16:15; 17:14) in which all would be brought to a fateful decision with permanent results."[4] William H. Shea observed an even larger correspondence: "All of the main elements of the latter [Armageddon] are paralleled in 1 Kings 18 in historically concrete form [Ahab, the king; Jezebel, his pagan wife; and the false prophets of Baal over against the prophet Elijah]."[5]

John's Apocalypse considers the wars of Israel's God to be local foreshadowings of the cosmic-universal battle of Armageddon. Israel's salvation history implies the assurance that once more, at the end of the church age, God will intervene on behalf of His faithful worshipers. At His second coming, Jesus will unveil His messianic splendor as the Warrior-King and vindicate His followers, while "the beast," "the false prophet," and their followers will be ashamed and perish (see Rev. 19:11-21).

To understand why God brings His last-plagues judgment on Babylon, we must define that entity from God's perspective. We should not define Babylon by her geographic location or ethnic composition, as popular theology tends to do, but by her relation to the

God of Israel and His people. In short, we must define Babylon purely *theologically*.

Revelation mentions Babylon only because of her hostility to the God of Israel and Zion, His true people. As I explained in an earlier publication:

> The essential characteristic of Babylon is plain—it was the arch-enemy of both Israel and her covenant God. It rejected the truth of saving grace as revealed in the sacred Temple of Jerusalem, blasphemed the God of Israel, and oppressed the people of God. Here we have the *theological* character of Babylon as religious type that continues in all her future manifestations, especially in her apocalyptic antitype during the time of the end. Babylon's defiance of God's authority has, therefore, two dimensions—vertically: against God's revealed will in His sanctuary; horizontally: against His covenant people and their forms of worship. Babylon is at war on both fronts because they are inseparably connected. The war against Yahweh, the God of Israel, is realized immediately in the war against the Israel of God. The principle of defiance that inspired Babylon of old will again motivate apocalyptic Babylon. But this event will inevitably ensure the same divine verdict on end-time Babylon as that executed on its historical types.[6]

The Fall of Babylon in Type and Antitype

The book of Revelation repeatedly assures readers that Babylon will be judged both in a judicial judgment in heaven (see Rev. 14:8) and by her destruction in the final plagues (14:9-11; 16:12-21; 17:16; 19:1-3). While justice requires Babylon's fall, however, that fall also serves a higher purpose: the deliverance of Israel. This release of the oppressed is what makes the doom of Babylon good news. Babylon's fall sets Israel free for her final exodus en route to Mount Zion in the New Jerusalem (14:1; 20:9). And just as God's judgment struck ancient Babylon with surprising suddenness (Isa. 47:9, 11; Jer. 51:8), so Jesus will bring a sudden judgment on the Babylon that is the kingdom of the antichrist (Rev. 18:8, 10, 19). But the fall of modern Babylon will be infinitely more devastating than that of its historical type: Modern Babylon will experience Armageddon.

The correspondence between the falls of ancient and modern Babylon calls for a careful consideration of the manner in which the ancient city was overthrown. The prophet Isaiah foretold that Babylon would fall as a consequence of a sudden "drying up" of the Euphrates river. This "drying up" of Babylon's river would prepare the way for Cyrus, the Persian general, and the allied kings from the East to enter the city by surprise and to conquer it (Isa. 41:2, 25; 44:27, 28).

The Greek historians Herodotus and Xenophon report that Cyrus did just that; he breached Babylon's defenses by diverting the flow of the Euphrates.[7] As a result, Babylon fell into the hands of the Persians "without any battle," as stated on the famous Cyrus cylinder found in the ruins of Babylon and now in the British Museum.[8]

So, the manner in which Babylon fell fulfilled Isaiah's prophecy literally. The Spirit of inspiration had even moved Isaiah to bestow on Cyrus the honorable titles of "anointed," or *messiah,* and "my shepherd" (Isa. 45:1; 44:28), titles that indicate that Cyrus's military victory over Babylon and his liberation of the Jews from their captors (Ezra 1:1-4) foreshadowed Jesus' mission at Armageddon. It was Yahweh who had spoken to the Euphrates: " 'Be dry, and I will dry up your streams' " (Isa. 44:27). Cyrus was merely God's agent in the judgment on Babylon. Just as God and His covenant people were at the center of the fall of ancient Babylon, so Jesus and His people stand at the center of the fall of modern Babylon at Armageddon.

To determine who constitute the Israel of God and who constitute Babylon in the end time, we must determine the theological character of each participant:

1) Babylon functioned as the enemy of the Lord and the oppressor of Israel.

2) The Euphrates was an integral part of Babylon, support-

ing and protecting it like a wall, and thus hostile to Israel.

3) The drying up of the Euphrates indicated God's judgment on Babylon and was the cause of its sudden downfall.

4) Cyrus and his allied kings of the Medes and the Persians (Jer. 50:41; 51:11, 28) came as the kings from the East to fulfill God's purpose for Babylon and Israel. They were the enemies of Babylon and the deliverers of Israel. Cyrus was "anointed" by the Lord to defeat Babylon and to set Israel free.

5) Daniel and Israel in Babylon were the repentant people of God, the faithful remnant of Israel (see Jer. 50:20).

These five religious characterizations of the fall of Babylon are the essentials that link type and antitype. In the book of Revelation, Babylon represents the archenemy of Jesus and of His church. Both Israel and Babylon are determined by their relation to Jesus. In the final stage of development, both Babylon and Israel have become universal, their territorial scope worldwide (see Rev. 14:6, 8). The final events will therefore be global in nature; the whole world comes under the spell of Babylon (13:3, 4, 7).

In harmony with this expansion of Babylon, Inspiration also gives to Babylon's river an explicitly worldwide application: " 'The waters you saw [the Euphrates], where the prostitute [Babylon] sits, are peoples, multitudes, nations and languages' " (Rev. 17:15). Those who insist that the Euphrates represents only the people who live in the actual geographic location of the literal river in the Middle East are bound to follow the same interpretation with Babylon, Israel, Mount Zion, and Armageddon. Those who do so fail to grasp the Christocentric character of biblical typology. The gospel of Jesus delivers the messianic age from the restrictions of ethnic and geographic literalism.

The Clarifying Role of Revelation 17

The angel who speaks to John in Revelation 17 is one of those who pour out the seven last plagues. His burden is to explain the " 'punishment of the great prostitute, who sits on many waters' " (v. 1).

Revelation 17, then, is meant to clarify the final plagues described in the previous chapter. Understanding this connection between chapters 17 and 16 is the key to correctly interpreting Armageddon as God's judgment on Babylon. Revelation 17 explains *how* God's judgment on Babylon will be realized. And the visions of chapters 18 and 19 continue to develop this theme—which means that Armageddon receives its definitive portrayal in Rev. 19:11-21.

Revelation 17 predicts an astounding reversal; Babylon's political leaders have provided wholehearted support for her religious leadership. Suddenly, that support disappears and is replaced by hate (vs. 16, 17). This chapter tells us that, surprisingly, God will bring about the destruction of Babylon *by way of her own supporters.* The "prostitute" will be handed over to her former lovers just as Ezekiel 16:37-41 predicted would happen to the "prostitute" Israel.* The waters of the Euphrates, which represent the multitudes that have supported Babylon in her apostasy and persecutions (Rev. 17:1, 2, 15), will suddenly "dry up"—that is, *suddenly withdraw their support.* Likewise, the ten-horned beast, which had been the harlot's illicit lover, will unexpectedly come to hate her and will destroy her completely: " 'The beast and the ten horns you saw will hate the prostitute. They will bring her to ruin and leave her naked; they will eat her flesh and burn her with fire' " (17:16). In God's providence, this sudden reversal of the long-standing union occurs at the very "hour" when Babylon plans to exterminate the worldwide remnant church of Jesus (see 12:17; 13:15-17; 16:13-16; 17:14).

Cyrus's diversion of the waters of the Euphrates prepared the way for the kings from the East to enter the capital of Babylon and to take over her world government. His historic liberation of Israel foreshadowed the coming of the greater Cyrus, the Messiah, or "Anointed One," who will descend from the cosmic East with "myriad" angels to rescue all who belong to Him by a living faith. This will fulfill Jesus' promise: " 'And he will send his angels with

*For a fuller treatment, see my *How to Understand the End-Time Prophecies of the Bible* (Sarasota, Florida: First Impressions, 1997), chapter 30.

a loud trumpet call, and they will gather his elect from the four winds, from one end of the heavens to the other' " (Matt. 24:31).

The celestial "kings from the sunrise" are as infinitely greater than their Old Testament type as Jesus is greater than Cyrus. Revelation 16 places the "kings from the East" (v. 12) in stark contrast with "the kings of the whole world" gathered together at Armageddon (vs. 13-16). This indicates that "the kings from the East" are not part of this world's political powers. They are the heavenly Liberators: the King of the universe, accompanied by Jesus and the angels of God. Angels are not kings in an earthly political sense. They are portrayed as riding "on white horses" and dressed in white as is Jesus Himself (Rev. 19:14). This indicates that God's angels participate in the same mission—the liberation of planet Earth—as does Jesus, the "KING OF KINGS" (19:16).

The ultimate purpose of Jesus' return is not the destruction of Babylon. It is the establishment of God's eternal reign of peace and justice on the earth, because Jesus is the Prince of Peace (see Isa. 9:6). Then "the earth will be full of the knowledge of the LORD as the waters cover the sea" (Isa. 11:9).

---

1. Rudolf Bultmann, *Theology of the New Testament* (New York: Charles Scribner's Sons, 1951), Vol. 1:288.

2. For an in-depth treatment, see my *The Israel of God in Prophecy: Principles of Prophetic Interpretation*, 10th ed. (Berrien Springs, Mich.: Andrews University Press, 1999).

3. D. P. Fuller, *Gospel and Law: Contrast or Continuum?* (Grand Rapids, Mich.: Eerdmans, 1980), 133.

4. s.v. "Armageddon," *The Anchor Bible Dictionary*, D. N. Freedman, ed. (New York: Doubleday, 1992).

5. "The Location and Significance of Armageddon in Revelation 16:16," *Andrews University Seminary Studies*, 18:2 (1980), 157-162.

6. Hans K. LaRondelle, *Chariots of Salvation: The Biblical Drama of Armageddon* (Hagerstown, Md.: Review & Herald, 1987), 87, 88.

7. See Herodotus, *Book I*, pp. 239, 240, and Xenophon, Cyropaedia 7.5.

8. See J. B. Pritchard, ed., *Ancient Near Eastern Texts*, 3rd ed. (Princeton, N.J.: Princeton University Press, 1969), 315.

Chapter Nine

THE SIGNIFICANCE OF THE MILLENNIUM

The approach of the third millennium of the church age has made the significance of the millennium in Revelation 20 a burning issue. People have proposed various theories about John's prediction of a thousand years of blessing for the resurrected saints, among them those theories now called "premillennialism," "postmillennialism," and "amillennialism." These designations indicate primarily their positions regarding the chronological relation of the millennium to Jesus' second coming. In other words, Bible students have disagreed as to whether Jesus will return at the beginning or the end of the millennium. Premillennialists, those who hold that Jesus' return will precede the millennium, differ among themselves as to the realm of His reign with His saints: Will they reign on earth or in heaven? And amillennialism simply accepts the thousand years as a symbol of an unspecified length of time. It can best be described as "inaugurated millennialism" because it considers the millennium to represent the entire Christian age between the two advents of Jesus.

Revelation 20 should be understood from its immediate context—that is, from the preceding vision, Revelation 19:11-21. That vision described the global impact of Jesus' second coming on the persecutors of His church: "The beast was captured, and with him the false prophet who had performed the miraculous signs on his behalf. . . . The two of them were thrown alive into the fiery lake of burning sulfur" (19:20). The description of their destruction raises the question as to what fate Armageddon brings to the third opponent among God's enemies, the mastermind of end-time Babylon—the dragon, Satan? The visions of 20:1-10 answer this question. So, the visions of 19:11-21 and 20:1-10 belong together logically and chronologically! To understand the time frame of the millennium, we must recognize these links.

Revelation 20:1-3 even provides a particular link with the Armageddon vision of Rev. 19:19, 20:

> I saw an angel coming down out of heaven, having the key to the Abyss and holding in his hand a great chain. *He seized the dragon, that ancient serpent, who is the devil, or Satan, and bound him for a thousand years.* He threw him into the Abyss, and locked and sealed it over him, *to keep him from deceiving the nations anymore* [Greek: *eti,* "any longer"] until the thousand years were ended. After that, he must be set free for a short time (Rev. 20:1-3).

In light of the union of the dragon, the beast, and the false prophet (see Rev. 16:13), this vision undoubtedly intends to picture what follows the events described in 19:19-21. After the beast and the false prophet were captured and thrown alive into the lake of burning sulfur at the Second Coming and all their followers were killed (19:20, 21), the dragon was seized and kept in the Abyss for a thousand years so that he can no longer deceive the nations (20:1-3). So, all three end-time enemies of Jesus who conspired to exterminate His church (16:13-16) are defeated. Two of them are executed at Armageddon, and Satan is captured and kept in remand to await trial.

While the Second Coming interrupts Satan's efforts to gather the nations to Armageddon, he will resume those efforts as soon as he is released at the millennium's end. John reveals:

When the thousand years are over, Satan will be released from his prison and will go out to deceive the nations in the four corners of the earth—Gog and Magog—to gather them for battle. . . . *And the devil, who deceived them, was thrown into the lake of burning sulfur, where the beast and the false prophet had been thrown* (Rev. 20:7, 8, 10).

The last sentence confirms the chronological order: the millennium follows Armageddon. It refers to the execution of the beast and his prophet in the lake of burning sulfur: an act that had taken place *before* the thousand years began (see Rev. 19:20). We agree therefore with the analysis of Richard A. Ostella:

The beast and the false prophet are apprehended in the very process of stimulating the battle of Armageddon through deception. Satan is apprehended in the same course of events; consequently, his deceptive activity must also include the process of stimulating the battle of Armageddon. . . . The deception of 20:1-3 is defined in the context of the unit extending from 19:11 through 20:3 as the deception which climaxes in the battle of Armageddon.[1]

Satan's capture at Armageddon marks the beginning of the millennium. His execution, however, takes place only after the millennium.

In addition to Revelation 19:11-21 and 20:1-10, we must recognize a third unit that is part of John's narrative here: the post-millennium judgment from the throne of God in which the wicked are raised to life to face the divine verdict and "the second death" (Rev. 20:11-15; 21:8). "If anyone's name was not found written in the book of life, he was thrown into the lake of fire" (20:15). Finally, "death and Hades were thrown into the lake of fire. The lake of fire is the second death" (20:14). All three units are "successively interlaced"[2] by connecting key terms: the frustrated efforts to deceive the nations (19:20; 20:3, 8), the thrones of judgment (20:4; 20:12), the heavenly city of the resurrected saints (20:9; 21:2-4).

In summary, Revelation 19:11–21:8 presents a close-knit literary unit that reveals three successive judgments: Armageddon, the millennium, and the Last Judgment. The over-arching theme of all three sections is the *Judgment and the second death,* which are progressively clarified (see the summation in 21:7-8). The literary composition of Revelation 19–21 demonstrates how dangerous it is to consider the millennium in isolation from its immediate context. From this context we learn that Jesus' second coming will cause the radical binding of Satan that marks the beginning of the millennium.

The Wider Context of the Book of Revelation

Augustine (A.D. 354-430) introduced what has become a popular view of the millennium in his epoch-making book *The City of God.* Revelation 20 speaks of Satan being bound and cast into the Abyss. Augustine proposed the theory that these actions may be identified with chapter 12's casting down of the dragon and so have already been accomplished by Jesus' first advent. He said the Abyss symbolizes the "non-Christian nations" and the thrones of judgment in Revelation 20:4 represent the ecclesiastical seats of the Roman bishops.[3]

Augustine's interpretation shifts the emphasis of the millennium away from the Second Advent and back to the first. It idealizes Rome as the Christian Zion. L. E. Froom comments: "This idea of the kingdom of God as the church ruling on earth was a sweeping, resplendent vision; but it was unbiblical, unsound, and misleading."[4] Augustine's understanding means that Revelation 20 presents just another recapitulation of church history rather than the climactic conclusion of the plan of salvation. His view became the standard interpretation, one that the mainline churches hold today.

We can test this view by comparing Revelation 20 to chapter 12, because chapter 12 presents a straightforward narrative of the church age. Interestingly, while both chapters deal with the dragon and the church, they demonstrate a clear chronological relationship. Chapter 12 tells of the dragon's attacks on the woman of God, his attempts to destroy the Messiah, his oppression of the saints for three and a half "times," and his preparation for his final war against the saints. Chapter 20, however, begins with the capture of Satan and his incapacitation so he can no longer deceive the nations. It concludes with his temporary release, which results, in turn, in his massive attack on "the camp of God's people" (20:9). Revelation 12ff tells of saints losing their lives because they have refused to accept the mark of the beast. By Revelation 20, these martyrs are resurrected saints: "They came to life and reigned with Christ a thousand years" (20:4).

Joel Badina sums up the progression from chapters 12 to 20:

First, in chapter 12, Satan is thrown down from heaven to earth, whereas in chapter 20 he is bound and thrown into the abyss (20:3). Second, in chapter 12 Satan is "the deceiver of the whole world" (12:9), whereas in chapter 20 he can "deceive the nations no more" (20:3). Third, chapter 12 portrays the Christians as martyrs put to death (12:11), whereas chapter 20 is the time of their resurrection (20:4, 6). Chapter 12 is a time of curse (12:12), whereas chapter 20 is a time of blessing (20:6). It is evident therefore, that chapters 12 and 20 do not describe the same period of time, and 20:1 does not go back to the first century A.D. as 12:1 does. Rather, 20:1-10 is to be located immediately subsequent to the Christian era.[5]

This comparison leads us to conclude that the millennium of Revelation 20 does not recapitulate the church age. The millennium succeeds the church era and begins with the glorious advent of Jesus and the resurrection of the saints.

The Present and the Future "Binding" of Satan
Just as there is a basic difference between the present and the

future salvation of the Christian, so there is a difference between the present and the apocalyptic "binding" of Satan. Revelation 20:7 tells of Satan's being temporarily released from bondage. How could this be true of any bondage accomplished by Jesus' crucifixion? Is not what Jesus accomplished on the cross finished once and forever?

The New Testament makes a clear distinction between Satan's expulsion from heaven by the cross of Jesus (see Rev. 12:10; John 12:31) and Satan's binding by the Second Advent (Rev. 20:1-3). At His first advent, Jesus broke Satan's dominion over humankind (see Col. 2:15). He said: " 'If I drive out demons by the Spirit of God, then the kingdom of God has come upon you. . . . How can anyone enter a strong man's house and carry off his possessions unless he first ties up the strong man? Then he can rob his house' " (Matt. 12:28, 29). Here Jesus demonstrated the kingdom of God *without its glorious consummation.* Jesus severely curtailed Satan's power over humanity because He is stronger than "the strong one" (Satan)! "In this basic sense the ministry of Jesus is the beginning of eschatological deliverance, the turning point of the aeons."[6] John's Apocalypse presupposes this spiritual kingdom of Jesus, yet it points forward also to Jesus' return as the victorious King of kings and Lord of lords (Rev. 17:14; 19:16), when He will seize the dragon, throw him into the Abyss, lock him up and seal him there so he can no longer do anything! (20:1-3).

Not only does the *time* of Satan's binding differ in Revelation 20 from that portrayed in the Gospels, but its *nature* differs also. At the Second Advent, Satan personally will be bound—confined to the abyss of a ruined world so that he can no longer deceive anyone. This portrays Satan's radical isolation in a locked and sealed pit. Every effort to relativize this apocalyptic imprisonment by placing it within church history denies the absolute nature of Satan's binding. G. C. Berkouwer asked "whether this sort of [relativizing] interpretation really does justice to the radical proportions of the binding of Satan—that he will not be freed from imprisonment for a thousand years."[7]

And Robert Mounce saw implied not just a curbing of Satan's activities but "the complete cessation of his influence on earth."[8]

The undeniable fact remains that centuries after the cross, Satan and his false apostles can still deceive the world by blinding the minds of unbelievers to the gospel (see 2 Cor. 4:4; 11:13, 14; 2 Thess. 2:9, 10). The devil still "prowls around like a roaring lion" (1 Pet. 5:8) and "is now at work in those who are disobedient" (Eph. 2:2). Even after his moral defeat at Jesus' crucifixion (Col. 2:15), Satan still successfully "leads the whole world astray" (Rev. 12:9; 13:14; 19:20). John wrote: "The whole world is under the control of the evil one" (1 John 5:19). Is this the picture of Satan bound so that he cannot deceive the world? The cross stripped Satan of all his rights before God, but not of his power to deceive humankind. Only the Second Advent will deprive him of that power, as the visions of Revelation 19–20 portray.

Israel's Prophets Provide the Key

Two Hebrew prophets, Daniel and Ezekiel, describe a sequence of end-time events that matches that of Revelation 19–20. Daniel portrays the antichrist's persecution of the saints for three and a half "times," followed by a heavenly court session that will take away his power and completely destroy him (Dan. 7:25, 26). Only then will the saints receive the kingdom of glory (v. 27). Daniel 11:40–12:2 expands this with the revelation that the antichrist or "king of the north" will once again attack the saints in the "time of the end" but will "come to his end, and no one will help him" (11:44, 45). He will be defeated suddenly by the heavenly Michael, who will raise the dead "who sleep in the dust of the earth" and cause the righteous to "shine like the brightness of the heavens" (12:2, 3).

Revelation 12–20 repeats and clarifies this basic sequence of Daniel 7–12. Revelation 12 applies much of Daniel 7 to the Christian era and to the people of Christ. And Revelation 19 expands chapter 12 by disclosing that the remnant church (of Rev. 12:17) will be rescued by her heavenly Defender (19:11-21). When Jesus appears, the antichrist-beast and his deceiving prophet will be executed (19:19, 20), while the righteous dead will be resurrected to life immortal (20:4-6). Then Jesus' faithful witnesses will be given thrones of judgment (20:4). As in Daniel 7 and 12, the reign of the saints in Revelation 20 comes *after* the persecutions of the antichrist and after the imposition of the mark of the beast (20:4). If the mark of the beast and the destruction of the beast at the Second Advent still wait for their fulfillment, *then the millennial reign of the risen saints must also wait for its fulfillment.* Relating Daniel to the millennium of Revelation 20, Jack S. Deere concludes: "On the basis of Daniel 7 it is more natural to read Revelation 20:4-6 as part of a chronological progression in its larger context (19:11–20:15) than as a recapitulation."[9]

Comparing Ezekiel with the millennium of Revelation 20 produces even more evidence that the fulfillment of the millennial reign of the saints lies in the future. Derwood C. Smith concludes, "The structure of Ezekiel 37–48 has determined the structure of Revelation 20:1–22:5."[10] Indeed, Ezekiel 37 portrays the resurrection of the whole house of Israel (vs. 10-14), after which the messianic reign begins (vs. 22-24). The Messiah will rule the resurrected Israel of God (37:12–13, 24). Ezekiel 38–39 continue with the description of the final attack of "Gog, of the land of Magog" in the far north, on the peaceful messianic kingdom of Israel (38:1-11). Burning sulfur from heaven will destroy Gog when God fights His holy war and appears in His awesome glory (38:18-23; 39:6). In Ezekiel's vision, these events are followed by the new temple with the new presence of God (40–48) in a New Jerusalem that is called "THE LORD IS THERE" (48:35).

The parallels between Ezekiel 37–48 and Revelation 20–22 are apparent:

Ezekiel 37–48	Revelation 20–22
The resurrection of all Israel (37:10-14); David, the king Messiah, reigns (37:22-24).	"The first resurrection" of the blessed and holy ones (20:6); "They came to life and reigned with Christ a thousand years" (20:4).

Ezekiel 37–48	Revelation 20–22
Gog, of the land of Magog, will attack the messianic kingdom of Israel, but will be destroyed by fire from heaven in God's last holy war (38:18-23; 39:6).	The end of the millennium is followed by the resurrection of "the rest of the dead" (20:5). Satan deceives these people into surrounding "the camp of God's people," the city of God. "But fire came down from heaven and devoured them" (20:7-9).
A new temple in Jerusalem becomes the place where God dwells eternally with Israel and the alien settlers (43:1-7; 44:4; 47:22, 23; 48:35).	The Holy City, the New Jerusalem, descends from heaven to earth as the eternal dwelling place of God and the Lamb with all humankind (21:1-5; 22:1-5).

These parallels indicate that John modeled his grand finale of the great controversy on that of Ezekiel. But John was a creative interpreter of Ezekiel. One scholar concluded that John presented a masterful "simplification and condensation of Ezekiel 40–48 in Revelation 21–22, . . . a tightly written, condensed summary of scriptures, reinterpreted and woven together into a new entity . . . to assure the first readers and hearers that all of their fondest hopes will be realized in the new heaven and the new earth."[11]

If John modeled his Apocalypse on Ezekiel, then an understanding of his use of that book is important for our interpretation of the millennium. The amillennial view fails because it ignores John's dependence on Ezekiel's outline. Ezekiel placed the final rebellion of the nations under Gog *after* the messianic kingdom (chapters 38–39). When the cleansing fire from heaven has devoured that rebellion, it purifies the earth, preparing it to receive the New Jerusalem (Ezek. 40–48). Thus, Ezekiel presents the clearest outline of eschatological events in the Old Testament. This means that "the reinterpretation of Ezekiel in the Book of Revelation . . . is the key to understanding the message of the book altogether."[12] (Of course, as we noted above, Daniel also supplies important background to Revelation.)

The Millennial Kingdom of Jesus

John describes his main vision of the millennium as follows:

> I saw thrones, and they sat upon them, and judgment was given to them. And I *saw* the souls of those who had been beheaded because of the testimony of Jesus and because of the word of God, and those who had not worshiped the beast or his image, and had not received the mark upon their forehead and upon their hand; and they came to life and reigned with Christ for a thousand years. The rest of the dead did not come to life until the thousand years were completed. This is the first resurrection. Blessed and holy is the one who has a part in the first resurrection; over these the second death has no power, but they will be priests of God and of Christ and will reign with Him for a thousand years (Rev. 20:4-6, NASB).

This remarkable vision predicts that the kingship of Jesus will last for a "thousand years" beyond the Second Coming. "Consequently, the thousand-year kingdom should be identified neither with the whole chronological extent of Jesus' lordship nor with the present Church."[13] Revelation 20 does not contain the slightest hint that the millennial reign of Jesus is on earth or over a Jewish kingdom. John sees the millennial reign of the risen saints *in heaven;* they are seated on thrones in heaven, not on earth. They reign with Christ, and they are where Jesus and His throne are—in heaven (3:21; 15:2).

Some have tried to explain the "souls" of those who were beheaded because of the testimony of Jesus as souls without bodies, and therefore as "picturing deceased saints reigning in heaven and not on earth."[14] But John saw the "souls of those who had been slain because of the word of God" *"under the altar,"* waiting for their vindication (Rev. 6:9)—and thus not yet seated on thrones or "reigning in heaven" or "translated to heaven at death"![15] This proves that what John described in Revelation 20 follows what happened in chapter 6. In fact, the idea that the soul has some non-corporeal existence is not even a biblical concept but a Greek philosophical idea foreign to Hebrew thinking. There is no soul-body dichotomy in Scripture. In Revelation 20 John sees simply that those who had been beheaded come to life again and sit on thrones. The contrast is between life and death, glory and shame, justice and unrighteousness.

Comparing the throne scene in Revelation 20 with the heavenly throne scene in Daniel 7:9-14 suggests that Revelation 20 also refers to a heavenly court. Both Daniel 7 and Revelation 20 portray judgment scenes with thrones in heaven. In Daniel 7 God vindicates the persecuted saints: "The Ancient of Days came and pronounced judgment *in favor of the saints of the Most High*" (v. 22; cf. 12:1). In Revelation 20 these same saints are seated with Jesus on thrones and are given the authority to judge their persecutors (v. 4). This vision presents a noticeable progression in salvation history, which indicates that the heavenly court session in Revelation 20 succeeds the one in Daniel 7. The "souls" who requested God's judgment in Revelation 6:9, 10 *have* been vindicated and *have* come to life in the first resurrection in Revelation 20. During the millennium the executed ("beheaded") saints, together with Jesus, are the judges of their former persecutors. Paul's words apply here: "Do you not know that the saints will judge the world? . . . Do you not know that we will judge angels?" (1 Cor. 6:2, 3).

Revelation 20 provides the ultimate consolation for the maligned saints. God's verdict will completely reverse their "defeat" and death: "Blessed and holy are those who have part in the first resurrection" (Rev. 20:6). This magnificent beatitude indicates that not only martyrs but all faithful Christians are included in the first resurrection. John said, "They came to life [Greek: *ezêsan*] and reigned with Christ a thousand years" (20:4). What does this expression—they "came to life"—mean? Was John speaking of a bodily resurrection or a spiritual resurrection? Here lies another key to understanding the millennium. The first resurrection is promised as the reward for those who died as martyrs or remained faithful to the testimony of

Jesus till the end (20:4). Believers are already spiritually reborn. Therefore, this resurrection must be their bodily resurrection.

As the counterpart of their resurrection, we read: "The rest of the dead did not come to life [Greek: *ouk ezêsan*] until the thousand years were ended" (Rev. 20:5). The meaning is evident; John wrote here of a literal resurrection of the rest of the dead. Both resurrections in Revelation 20:4, 5 are of the same kind, referring to literal resurrections. Isbon T. Beckwith states: "The new spiritual life in Christ cannot be thought of here; the context shows that the revival from physical death is meant."[16] This implies that those who participate in the second resurrection are the wicked and unholy ones, destined for the second death. They are raised to face the judgment "according to what they had done as recorded in the books" (20:12) because their names were not found written in the book of life (20:15).

The Millennium Rooted in Isaiah 24
Many have recognized that Isaiah 24:21, 22 is the particular Old Testament root of the millennium of Revelation 20. G. R. Beasley-Murray states: "The essential idea of Revelation 19:19–21:3 is present in brief compass in Isaiah 24:21f."[17] The connection between Revelation 20 and Isaiah 24 is instructive regarding the state of the earth during the millennium—the scene is one of utter desolation; the earth is a global graveyard, a worldwide Abyss.

The LORD is going to lay waste the earth and devastate it. . . . The floodgates of the heavens are opened, the foundations of the earth shake. The earth is broken up, the earth is split asunder, the earth is thoroughly shaken. . . . In that day the LORD will punish the powers in the heavens above and the kings on the earth below. They will be herded together like prisoners bound in a dungeon; they will be shut up in prison and be punished after many days (Isa. 24:1, 18, 19, 21, 22).

Isaiah's vision reveals that God's final judgment contains progressive stages: At God's appearance the evil powers of heaven and earth will be seized but not immediately punished. They will be "shut up in prison" and be punished *after many days*—that is, after an unspecified period of imprisonment. This is indeed the germinal concept of the millennium on earth, where Satan will be bound in the bottomless pit or dungeon of the earth for a thousand years.

Isaiah described Satan as a multiheaded serpent-dragon (Isa. 27:1), thus establishing another link of the Isaiah Apocalypse (chaps. 24–27) with Revelation 20 (v. 2). And Isaiah assured that "in that day" the faithful dead of Israel will be resurrected bodily from the dust (Isa. 26:19) and will be gathered to Mount Zion for the great banquet of the LORD with a loud trumpet blast (25:6-8; 27:13). In Revelation this banquet becomes "the wedding supper of the Lamb," when the bride, the church of all ages, will be united forever with her Redeemer (Rev. 19:6-9). This wedding feast takes place *in heaven* during the millennium, after all the martyrs and faithful ones have come to life in the first resurrection (20:4, 5). Jesus promised His disciples that He would return to take them to His "Father's house," so that they would be where He is (see John 14:1-3).

Most people do not realize that during the millennium all people on earth are dead: "The rest of the dead did not come to life until the thousand years were ended" (Rev. 20:5). This will be the result of the consuming power of the glorious Parousia of the heavenly Warrior, as Revelation 19 foretells: "The rest of them were killed with the sword that came out of the mouth of the rider on the horse, and all the birds gorged themselves on their flesh" (v. 21). This vision speaks of the death of *all* unbelievers. It is this universal result of the Parousia (see also Rev. 6:14-17; 16:17-21) that "binds" Satan to a desolate earth, leaving him unable to deceive anyone until the thousand years are ended. Only in Revelation 20:12 are these dead raised to life to stand before the throne. Between chapter 19 and 20:12 all people on earth are dead, as stated explicitly in 20:5. So there will be no "nations" on earth to rule over during the millennium.

Does Isaiah 65 Refer to the Millennium?

The assumption of the New Scofield Reference Bible that Isaiah 65:18-25 must be applied literally to the "millennial conditions in the renewed earth"[18] is not warranted. The new covenant has made the old covenant "obsolete" (Heb. 8:13) because Jesus has set it "aside" "to establish the second"(Heb. 10:9). This change is fundamental to the Christian faith. Isaiah 65–66 are not the *final* word of God! We must understand these visions of future glory in the light of Jesus' new covenant.

Revelation 21–22 function as the inspired expansion of Isaiah 65–66, as a more glorious fulfillment than the old covenant expected. The risen Lord enlarged Isaiah's limited view, which still included death (see Isa. 65:20). He made a better promise, one in which death and sin no longer exist in God's kingdom on the earth made new: " 'There will be no more death or mourning or crying or pain, for the old order of things has passed away' " (Rev. 21:4). The fulfillment will be *greater* than a literal reading of the old promises, as Isaiah himself had suggested: " 'The former things will not be remembered, nor will they come to mind.' " (Isa. 65:17; see also 1 Cor. 2:9). Revelation 21 cites and transforms Isaiah's portrayals (65:17, 19) by applying them to a more perfect earth than Isaiah described (Rev. 21:1, 4).

Why did God place an intermediate period between the Second Advent and the earth made new? This period does more than merely allow time for the rehabilitation of the persecuted followers of Jesus. It sees the vindication of God Himself in all His verdicts and judgments on sin and sinners. The risen saints' assessments of the divine judgments will place the wisdom, justice, and goodness of both the Father and the Son forever beyond question. All creatures in heaven and on earth, the righteous and the wicked, cannot but bow their knees at the name of Jesus and "confess that Jesus Christ is Lord, to the glory of God the Father" (Phil. 2:10, 11). All those around the throne of God respond with a sevenfold doxology: " 'Worthy is the Lamb, who was slain, to receive power and wealth and wisdom and strength and honor and glory and praise!' " (Rev. 5:12).

According to Israel's laws, a malicious witness whom the judges found, after "a thorough investigation," to have falsely accused someone of a crime was sentenced to suffer the very punishment the accused faced (Deut. 19:18-20). This "thorough investigation" may well be the task assigned the glorified saints during the millennium (see Rev. 20:4; 1 Cor. 6:2, 3). At the end, all judges will be profoundly satisfied and express as their deepest conviction:

"Great and marvelous are your deeds, Lord God Almighty. Just and true are your ways, King of the ages. Who will not fear you, O Lord, and bring glory to your name? For you alone are holy. All nations will come and worship before you, *for your righteous acts have been revealed*" (Rev. 15:3, 4).

In the gift of His Son as an atoning sacrifice for all people God's unselfish love and justice stand before the entire cosmos, eternally eliciting their adoration, praise, and worship!

1. *The Westminster Theological Journal* 37 (1975), 238.
2. Giblin, *Biblica*, 55, (1974), 500.
3. Augustine, *The City of God*, Bk. xx, 9.
4. *The Prophetic Faith of Our Fathers* (Hagerstown, Md.: Review & Herald, 1950), 1:489.
5. "The Millennium," in *Symposium on Revelation*, Frank Holbrook, ed. (Silver Spring, Md.: Biblical Research Institute, 1992), bk. II:236.
6. D. A. Hagner, *Matthew 1-13* (Dallas, Tex.: Word Biblical Commentary, 1993), Vol. 33A:344.
7. *The Return of Christ* (Grand Rapids, Mich.: Eerdmans, 1972), 305.
8. *The Book of Revelation* (Grand Rapids, Mich.: Eerdmans, 1977), 353.
9. *Biblica Sacra* 135 (1978), 61.
10. "The Millennial Reign of Jesus Christ: Some Observations on Rev. 20:1-10," *Restoration Quarterly* 16 (1973), 1:223.
11. J. Vogelgesang, *The Interpretation of Ezekiel in the Book of Revelation*, Ph.D. Diss., Harvard Univ., 1985 (Ann Arbor, Mich.: University Microfilms, Inc., 1987), 120-122.
12. Ibid., 394.

13. Oscar Cullmann, *The Christology of the New Testament* (Philadelphia: The Westminster Press, 1963), 226.
14. G. K. Beale, *The Book of Revelation,* New International Greek Testament Commentary (Grand Rapids, Mich.: Eerdmans, 1999), 998.
15. Ibid., 996.
16. *The Apocalypse of John* (Grand Rapids, Mich.: Baker, 1979), 740.
17. *Revelation* (Grand Rapids, Mich.: Eerdmans, 1983), 286.
18. New Scofield Reference Bible (1967), page 768.

Chapter Ten

A NEW JERUSALEM ON A NEW EARTH

John ends the Apocalypse of Jesus Christ with a splendid vision of the descent of the New Jerusalem from heaven to earth (Rev. 21–22). This completes the series of visions that began with the glorious return of Jesus to rescue His people from Armageddon (19:11-21). Thus John's vision of the visible glory of God's presence on earth forms the climax of the entire Apocalypse; finally, God will be "all in all" (1 Cor. 15:28).

Revelation 21–22 binds all the rest of the book together, especially the sections on the church militant (chaps. 2–3) and the church triumphant (chaps. 21–22). These chapters offer the struggling church the most sublime encouragement. George B. Caird declared, "In some ways this is the most important part of his book, as it is certainly the most familiar and beloved. . . . Here is the real source of John's prophetic certainty."[1]

The significance of the New Jerusalem vision stands out more clearly when we observe its sharp contrast to the judgment vision of Babylon, "the great prostitute" who has committed "adultery" with

143

the kings of the earth (Rev. 17:1, 2). The deliberate contraposition becomes apparent when the angel who has the seven bowl plagues shows John both the punishment of Babylon and the blessing of the New Jerusalem:

Revelation 17:1, 2	Revelation 21:9
One of the seven angels who had the seven bowls came and said to me, *"Come, I will show you the punishment of the great prostitute. . . .* With her the kings of the earth committed adultery."	One of the seven angels who had the seven bowls full of the seven last plagues came and said to me, *"Come, I will show you the bride, the wife of the Lamb."*

John borrows the Hebrew images of the Lord's "wife" and of "the prostitute" from Isaiah and Ezekiel to show that God's covenant with Israel will find an end-time fulfillment far beyond all expectations. His intentional counterpoint suggests that humankind faces only two possible destinies: either we will share in the punishment of Babylon or we will enjoy the eternal glory of the New Jerusalem. These destinies depend on our choice either to follow God and remain loyal to Jesus or to compromise with Babylon, the great prostitute, the unfaithful church.

The Essence of John's Jerusalem Visions

In Revelation 21–22, John describes two visions of the New Jerusalem (21:1-8; 21:9–22:5). The second, more detailed vision clarifies the first. This arrangement indicates that John has presented the essence of humanity's eternal destiny in Revelation 21:1-8. We will therefore focus primarily on that vision and look for further clarification in the description that follows.

I saw a new heaven and a new earth, for the first heaven and the first earth had passed away, and there was no longer any sea. I saw the Holy City, the new Jerusalem, coming down out of heaven from God, prepared as a bride beautifully dressed for her husband. And I heard a loud voice from the throne saying,

"Now the dwelling of God is with men, and he will live with them. They will be his people, and God himself will be with them and be their God. He will wipe every tear from their eyes. There will be no more death or mourning or crying or pain, for the old order of things has passed away."

He who was seated on the throne said, "I am making everything new!" Then he said, "Write this down, for these words are trustworthy and true." He said to me: "It is done. I am the Alpha and the Omega, the Beginning and the End. To him who is thirsty I will give to drink without cost from the spring of the water of life. He who overcomes will inherit all this, and I will be his God and he will be my son. But the cowardly, the unbelieving, the vile, the murderers, the sexually immoral, those who practice magic arts, the idolaters and all liars—their place will be in the fiery lake of burning sulfur. This is the second death" (Rev. 21:1-8).

This climactic vision is not a totally new creation. Nearly every phrase of John's description of his New Jerusalem vision in some way or another grows out of God's promises to Israel, restructured here to fit a Christ-centered and universal perspective. This surprising convergence of so many Old Testament promises assures the Christian readers and hearers that all Israel's hopes will be gloriously realized through Jesus in the earth made new.

The Old Testament Connection
Through Jesus, God provided a new revelation that makes the New Testament the ultimate authority of His covenant promises (see Heb. 1:1, 2). This Testament elevates the New Jerusalem as "the bride, the wife of the Lamb" (Rev. 21:2, 9). The Christological fulfillment in the people of Jesus transcends an isolated, literal reading of the Old Testament. Jesus is the "guarantee of a better covenant" (Heb. 7:22).

We can feel the full impact of John's visions of the New Jerusalem when we relate them to Israel's covenant promises. We must connect

John's visions with the hopes of the Hebrew prophets to determine the basic continuity as well as the wider perspective revealed in the Apocalypse of Jesus Christ. The two primary sources of Revelation 21–22 are the prophecies of Isaiah (chaps. 25; 54; 60–62; 65; 66) and of Ezekiel (chaps. 40–48).

Isaiah recorded these promises of Israel's God:

"Behold, I will create new heavens and a new earth. The former things will not be remembered, nor will they come to mind. . . . I will rejoice over Jerusalem and take delight in my people; the sound of weeping and of crying will be heard in it no more." (Isa. 65:17, 19; see also 66:22).

Clearly, John's description in Revelation 21:1-5 repeats Isaiah's promises in an abridged form. Yet John does more than that. He also gives Isaiah's hope a fresh perspective: "There will be no more death or mourning or crying or pain, for the old order of things [Greek: *ta prôta,* "the first things"] has passed away" (Rev. 21:4). This assurance from the throne of God surpasses the promises of Isaiah, in whose new heavens and earth death still plays a part (see Isa. 65:20). (Though Isaiah's apocalyptic forecast in chapters 24–27 does include the promise that God "will swallow up death forever. The Sovereign LORD will wipe away the tears from all faces; he will remove the disgrace of his people from all the earth" [Isa. 25:8].) A life without death, grief, tears, and pain (Rev. 21:4) requires a new creative act of God for humanity and the world. It cannot be the outcome of human technology or medical science.

John emphasizes that the old cosmos will disappear completely when God's throne becomes visible to human beings: "Earth and sky [Greek: *ouranos,* "heaven"] fled from his presence" (Rev. 20:11). And the dangerous sea, as we know it, will no longer exist (21:1). A new creation will replace the dissolution of the old one. John uses the word *kainos,* or "new," in the sense of "a new kind" of heaven and earth. It will be a radically transformed earth, comparable perhaps with the human body that will be raised in new glory without losing its former identity. The mystery of the new remains, because God as Creator announces: " 'I am making everything new!' " (21:5). His creative acts exceed all human expectations: " 'No eye has seen, no ear has heard, no mind has conceived what God has prepared for those who love him' " (1 Cor. 2:9). Jesus called this glorious future " 'the renewal [Greek: *palingenesia,* "regeneration"] of all things' " (Matt. 19:28).

We can see Isaiah's influence in Revelation's statements that God will create a new heaven and earth. But in developing the grand finale of his Apocalypse, John relied even more heavily on the visions of Ezekiel, whose motifs he used systematically to develop the layout of his book (in chaps. 4–5; 7; 10; 17–20). Vogelgesang, who points this out, shows that John did not follow Ezekiel slavishly but uses his material creatively.[2] For instance, while John made detailed use of Ezekiel's visions of the new temple (chaps. 40–48) in constructing his New Jerusalem vision, Revelation 21:22 stress that the holy city in which God will dwell *has no temple!* In the New Jerusalem, the throne of God and of the Lamb replaces the temple. Here John has deliberately reinterpreted Ezekiel's prophecy. (We will look at this in more detail later.)

The Holy City, the New Jerusalem

John sees the glorified people of God not as a shapeless multitude, but as a well-ordered community, as a "city." As a *"holy* city," it represents righteousness and peace because God dwells in its midst. Peace means more than the absence of war; it signifies the presence of God.

This city will be home to many ethnic groups and cultures because "the glory and honor of the nations will be brought into it" (Rev. 21:26). The Creator redeems people personally and still characterized by their own culture. This points beyond the isolated communion of the soul with God. In the new world, people will encounter God within the fellowship of others.

In the book of Revelation the New Jerusalem is called "the bride, the wife of the Lamb" (Rev. 21:9). This tells us that the future city belongs to Jesus. He created it, and He will maintain it into all eternity. As a visible sign of His care He gives all its citizens the right to eat from the "tree of life" and to drink from the "water of life" that flows from the throne of God and of the Lamb (see 22:1, 2, 17). Humanity's dependence on God, the Creator, continues. The risen Jesus guarantees the eternal life of the redeemed:

> The throne of God and of the Lamb will be in the city, and his servants will serve him (Rev. 22:3).
> He who sits on the throne will spread his tent over them. Never again will they hunger; never again will they thirst. . . . For the Lamb at the center of the throne will be their shepherd; he will lead them to springs of living water. And God will wipe away every tear from their eyes. (Rev. 7:15-17).

The book of Revelation stresses continually that the Lamb cannot for a moment be separated from God. This comforting thought comes with peculiar force to the final generation in the protecting seal they receive: the 144,000 followers of the Lamb "had his name and his Father's name written on their foreheads" (Rev. 14:1).

And the name of the holy city, the "New Jerusalem," is itself very significant. It points to the basic continuity of the eternal future of all humanity with Israel's history. In spite of apostasy and rebellion, Jerusalem remained the guardian of the sacred words and covenant promises of God (see Rom. 3:3; 9:3-5).

The core of God's covenant promises was "I will be there. I will be your God and you will be my people." This promise was given to Moses (Exod. 25:8; Lev. 26:11, 12), was experienced in Israel's temple songs (Pss. 27; 46; 48; 63), and was renewed by the prophets (Hag. 2:9; Zech. 3; 8:3-8; Ezek. 40–48; Mal. 3). Ezekiel had prophesied that during the messianic age God would restore His covenant with a spiritually renewed Israel (Ezek. 37:14, 24). Through him, God said of spiritual Israel, " 'My dwelling place will be with them; I will be their God, and they will be my people' " (37:27).

The New Testament applies this same promise to Jesus and to the people He has called out from among all nations: "We are the temple of the living God" (2 Cor. 6:16; cf. Eph. 2:19-22). As a result, the witness is given "if anyone is in Christ, he is a new creation; the old has gone, the new has come!" (2 Cor. 5:17). This transforming power comes from Jesus, who testified: " 'I tell you that one greater than the temple is here' " (Matt. 12:6; cf. also John 2:19). He could say: " 'I and the Father are one. . . . Anyone who has seen me has seen the Father' " (John 10:30; 14:9). By believing in Jesus we can enter God's dwelling place even in this age. From Jesus we receive the rest of grace, peace with God, and the messianic joy (Matt. 11:28; John 14:27; 15:11).

The City Without a Temple

When the New Jerusalem descends from heaven to earth, God says, " 'Now the dwelling [Greek: *skênê,* "tabernacle, sanctuary"] of God is with men, and he will live with them. They will be his people, and God himself will be with them and be their God' " (Rev. 21:3). But John writes, "I did not see a temple in the city, because the Lord God Almighty and the Lamb are its temple" (21:22). This statement probably shocked its Jewish readers. However, the temple promise of Israel's prophets will be fulfilled more gloriously than they ever dared to think.

The ultimate blessing of the inhabitants of the Holy City grows out of their beatific vision: "They will see [God's] face, and his name will be on their foreheads" (Rev. 22:4). The redeemed will enjoy the unprecedented blessing of unhindered access to God and Jesus, and this unmediated communion will bring the highest elation and rapture of the human soul! This circumstance also explains why neither a temple nor a special priesthood will ever be needed in the New Jerusalem. The fact that the eternal home of the redeemed has no temple is the very consummation of the temple idea: all who live in the city will see God in His glory. The entire city is now the Most Holy Place—the place where God dwells! The shape of the city represents this idea; John describes it as a cube: "He measured the city with the rod and found it to be 12,000 stadia in length, and as wide and high as it is long" (21:16). That was the shape of the Most Holy Place in Israel's temple (1 Kings 6:20).

The size of the New Jerusalem represents its unimaginable greatness: 12,000 stadia equals about 1,500 miles! A cube of that height would reach far beyond the ionosphere. The number 12 appears not only in the dimensions of the city but also in the number of its gates and foundations (Rev. 21:12-17). Apparently, that number was meant to help us understand the meaning of the cube, its walls, gates, and foundations. The gates of the New Jerusalem are named for the 12 tribes of Israel, God's Old Testament people. And its foundations are named for the twelve apostles, the spiritual progenitors of His New Testament people. So, the New Jerusalem embraces all true followers of God (21:12-14). His holy city will be the home of redeemed humanity as a whole. It will be the only universal city of all human history.

Two features of the city stress its inclusiveness: First, the city is open to all directions of the compass. The three gates on each of the four sides invite all to enter, because "on no day will its gates ever be shut" (Rev. 21:13, 25). This expresses unlimited access. Second, God Himself declares (in "a loud voice from the throne") that now His dwelling "is with men. . . . They will be his *peoples* [plural in older mss]" (21:3). The term *peoples* indicates that the New Jerusalem is neither a Jewish nor a Gentile city but a universal city that includes all races, nations, and languages. Other statements give further emphasis to this concept: "The nations will walk by its light, and the kings of the earth will bring their splendor into it" (21:24); "The glory and honor of the nations will be brought into it" (21:26). This universal perspective implies that even former enemies of God and His people, from Babylon, Edom, Moab, Ammon, et cetera, are welcome in the eternal city of God (see also Zech. 14:16).

We can find the roots of this idea in Isaiah's prophecies of the worldwide influence of the old Jerusalem in the messianic age. God intended that "all nations" would "stream to it" and seek the spiritual guidance of the God of Israel (Isa. 2:1-5). He said,

> "Nations will come to your light, and kings to the brightness of your dawn. Lift up your eyes and look about you: All assemble and come to you; . . . the wealth on the seas will be brought to you, to you the riches of the nations will come" (Isa. 60:3-5).

But here, as elsewhere, John's vision exceeds that of Isaiah. That Old Testament prophet foresaw the kings of the Gentile nations being led into Jerusalem as captives (Isa. 60:11, 12, 14). John, however, sees them entering the New Jerusalem by their own choice, because of their faith in the Messiah of Israel. He sees the Gentile kings bring their "splendor" and the nations their "glory and honor" (Rev. 21:24, 26), which means primarily their "praise" and devotion, to God and the Lamb (see Isa. 60:6) rather than to Babylon (see Rev. 18:9-19).

With his inclusiveness, however, John retains also an essential characteristic of Ezekiel's prophetic vision of the temple: its *holiness*, symbolized by a surrounding wall that separates the holy from the profane (see Ezek. 42:20, NASB; cf. 44:23). Ezekiel's temple provided room for the priests alone (Ezek. 44:16). The New Jerusalem vision invites *everyone* who is thirsty to come to the throne of God in the city (Rev. 22:17). But it also mentions a fundamental condition for the blessed ones: " 'Blessed are those who wash their robes, that they may have the right to the tree of life and may go through the gates into the city' " (22:14). An angel clarifies this symbolic expression: " 'They have washed their robes and made them white in the blood of the Lamb' " (7:14). This vital condition points to our responsibility to acknowledge Jesus Christ as our personal Savior and to exercise our faith in Him by communing with Him daily, claiming His atoning death for the forgiveness of our sins and the cleansing of our consciences. This is what John meant by the continuous "washing of our robes" (22:14 has the present tense: "are washing"; see also 1 John 1:7-9; 2:1; Heb. 9:14; 10:19-22).

Babylon: the Counterpoint of the New Jerusalem

John contrasts the "wife of the Lamb" (Rev. 21:9), the New Jerusalem, with Babylon, the harlot city (17:1, 5). Significantly, Babylon is portrayed as an adulteress, or unfaithful married woman, who has intoxicated "the inhabitants of the earth . . . with the wine of her adulteries" (14:8; 17:2; 18:3; 19:2). From the time of Hosea (eighth century B.C.) the Old Testament prophets compared the relationship between God and His people to a marriage bond (Hos. 2:19, 20; Isa. 54:5). They condemned Israel's religious and moral apostasy in worshiping the gods of pagan nations as "prostitution" and "adulteries" (see Hos. 6:10; Jer. 3:1-3; and esp. Ezek. 16; 23). This background clarifies John's picture of the harlot Babylon. He describes God's destruction of Babylon in Revelation 17:16 in terms derived from Ezekiel 16:37-39, to the effect that her former, illicit lovers will unexpectedly become her destroyers. So, Ezekiel holds the key to understanding Revelation 17.

Babylon is not simply a secular nation; it is the place where God's people live and worship in the time of the end. The final appeal from heaven makes apparent the seriousness of this situation: " 'Come out of her, my people, so that you will not share in her sins, so that you will not receive any of her plagues; for her sins are piled up to heaven, and God has remembered her crimes' " (Rev. 18:4, 5).

This heavenly ultimatum applies with peculiar force to the last generation because they will witness the seven last plagues of Revelation 16. To indicate the right time for their exodus from Babylon, God will pour out His Spirit in its fullness on a global scale to complete the work that began at Pentecost with the apostles. John writes: "After this I saw another angel coming down from heaven. He had great authority, and *the earth was illuminated by his splendor*" (Rev. 18:1). Thus Babylon's moral fall will be exposed: her self-exaltation, unfaithfulness to Jesus, and horrible crimes against God's people (18:2-5). (Of the latter, John writes with astonishment: "I saw that the woman was drunk with the blood of the saints, the blood of those who bore testimony to Jesus" [17:6]. These are the martyrs that will enter the New Jerusalem [see 20:4].)

John describes Babylon as an unclean city and "a home for demons" (Rev. 18:2). Those who remain in Babylon "have not been written in the book of life" (17:8). In contrast, he says of the New Jerusalem: "Nothing impure will ever enter it, nor will anyone who does what is shameful or deceitful, but only those whose names are written in the Lamb's book of life" (21:27). While the harlot was dressed in purple and scarlet "and was glittering with gold, precious stones and pearls" (17:4), the Lamb's wife "shone with the glory of God, and its brilliance was like that of a very precious jewel, like a jasper, clear as crystal" (21:11). John mentions especially the wall, its twelve foundations and its twelve gates, each made of a single pearl (21:18-21). William W. Reader best explains its significance: "They symbolize the presence of God, the divine origin of the city, and the new people of God."[3] John thus deliberately contrasts the pearls of the "wife of the Lamb" to the jewels that adorn the harlot of Babylon (see also 17:4; 18:12, 16).*

John describes in detail the eternal destiny of Babylon, the doomed harlot city that tried to usurp God's throne and the New Jerusalem. God's verdicts determine their fate: a loud voice from the throne of God introduces the seventh bowl that destroys Babylon with the words "It is done!" (Rev. 16:17). And the eternal glory of the New Jerusalem becomes reality because God again says: " 'It is done!' " (21:6). John quotes an angel as saying " 'the great city of Babylon will be thrown down, never to be found again. . . . The light of a lamp will never shine in you again' " (18:21, 23). By contrast, he describes the New Jerusalem as the place where "there will be no more night. They will not need the light of a lamp or the light of the sun, for the Lord God will give them light. And they will reign for ever and ever" (22:5); "The Lamb is its lamp" (21:23).

The primary purpose of John's sustained contrast between pow-

---

*John's description of the New Jerusalem as built on foundations that carry the names of the twelve apostles (Rev. 21:14) indicates that God will found the new world not upon the patriarchs of Israel but upon the first witnesses to Jesus. Their testimony about Jesus is the absolute criterion of God's truth (see Rev. 20:4).

erful but doomed Babylon and the eternal New Jerusalem is to exhort the faltering saints of Revelation 2–3 to end their compromising with the apostate, worldly church and to choose instead faithfulness to God alone.

Divine Encouragement and Warning for Today

The New Jerusalem vision concludes with a direct message from Him who is seated on the throne: " 'I am making everything new! . . . Write this down, for these words are trustworthy and true' " (Rev. 21:5). The New Jerusalem is not an improved or rebuilt old Jerusalem; God will create a new Holy City. Abraham anticipated this: "He was looking forward to the city with foundations, whose architect and builder is God" (Heb. 11:10). He was fully convinced that "God had power to do what he had promised" (Rom. 4:21). And all of Abraham's children have been "longing for a better country—a heavenly one. Therefore God is not ashamed to be called their God, for he has prepared a city for them" (Heb. 11:16).

Peter's faith conveyed this apocalyptic hope to the apostolic church: "But in keeping with his [God's] promise we are looking forward to a new heaven and a new earth, the home of righteousness" (2 Pet. 3:13). He explained that the seeming delay of the day of judgment has a redemptive purpose: "The Lord is not slow in keeping his promise, as some understand slowness. He is patient with you, not wanting anyone to perish, *but everyone to come to repentance*" (2 Pet. 3:9). The fulfillment of God's promise is so certain that God declares concerning the new heaven and new earth " 'It is done' " (Rev. 21:6).

God's profound self-designation draws another nuance from this divine pledge: " 'I am the Alpha and the Omega, the Beginning and the End' " (Rev. 21:6; see also 1:8)—terminology that Jesus also used of Himself (see 22:13). These names mean that only in God and Jesus do human beings and world history receive their ultimate meaning. They express God's rulership over the world, reassuring us that He can bring humankind to the goal He has set: the New Jerusalem! God thus claims to guide the course of human history toward Paradise restored! His eternal purpose is the unshakable foundation of our hope.

Revelation assures us that God offers the followers of the Lamb a foretaste of heaven—that right now we may experience the redemptive powers of the age to come. God promises, " 'To him who is thirsty I will give to drink without cost from the spring of the water of life' " (Rev. 21:6). While this promise will be consummated in the New Jerusalem (22:1), it also assures thirsty souls a blessing now. The Spirit and the "bride" (the New Jerusalem) invite all people today with these words:

" 'Come!' Whoever is thirsty, let him come; and whoever wishes, let him take the free gift of the water of life" (Rev. 22:17).

God offered the grace of His fellowship to Israel when He called them out of ancient Babylon: " 'Come, all you who are thirsty, come to the waters; . . . Come, buy wine and milk without money and without cost' " (Isa. 55:1). Jewish tradition identified the metaphor of "water" with the Torah, or Hebrew Bible.[4] Jesus substituted instead fellowship with Himself, the Messiah: " 'Whoever drinks the water I give him will never thirst. Indeed, the water I give him will become in him a spring of water welling up to eternal life' " (John 4:14; see also 7:37-39). The "water of life" represents eternal fellowship with God and Jesus (see Jer. 2:13; Ps. 36:8, 9; John 4:10; 7:37). One cannot earn this fellowship by believing in certain doctrines or by moral rectitude. God offers it "without cost" (Rev. 21:6), as a "free gift" (22:17) to all who accept the Lamb of God and follow His testimony.

The glory of the New Jerusalem is pledged again in these words: " 'He who overcomes will inherit all this [the New Jerusalem and the new earth], and I will be his God and he will be my son' " (Rev. 21:7). The verb "to inherit" reaffirms the promise of life eternal "without cost" (21:6). The notion of an "inheritance" proves that we cannot earn the eternal city of God by our merits; it comes as God's gracious gift to His children. But the inheritance is promised only to those who "overcome." What does that mean?

From the seven letters to the churches we learn that to "overcome" means to persevere in our faith in Jesus, to follow Him even in times of apostasy and persecution. In other places in Revelation John describes this as "patient endurance and faithfulness" (Rev. 13:10) and as keeping "the commandments of God and [holding] fast the faith of Jesus" (14:12, NRSV). He portrays the last generation of believers as those who "follow the Lamb wherever he goes" and keep themselves from defilement: "No lie was found in their mouths; they are blameless" (14:1-5). " 'Overcomers' are those whose lives are characterized by refusal to compromise their faith despite the threat of persecution. They ironically conquer when they maintain their faith even though they appear defeated in the world's eyes because of persecution."[5]

Contrasting the overcomers with those who are excluded from the New Jerusalem dramatically clarifies their identity: " 'The cowardly, the unbelieving, the vile, the murderers, the sexually immoral, those who practice magic arts, the idolaters and all liars—their place will be in the fiery lake of burning sulfur. This is the second death' " (Rev. 21:8; see also 22:15). John's list of losers highlights the seven kinds of overcomers mentioned in chapters 2-3. From the first characteristic (cowardice) to the last (the lie), John's concern points to the high calling of the Christian to witness to Jesus and to follow Him in a life of Christlikeness.

When John writes of "the lie" (in Rev. 14:5; 21:8, 27; 22:15), he's pointing to the distortion of the truth about God and the Lamb, especially as taught by the beast and the false prophet (see 2 Thess. 2:8-12). Paul said of those who compromise the Christian faith: "They claim to know God, but by their actions they deny him" (Tit. 1:16). All who obdurately persevere in practicing a lie in worship and life will be excluded from God's presence eternally; that is the essence of their judgment (Matt. 7:23; 25:41).

In this time of the end in which we live, God still offers forgiveness. Ultimately, overcomers are those who daily " 'wash their robes' " and therefore " 'have the right to the tree of life and may go through the gates into the city' " (Rev. 22:14).

The invitation to become citizens of that city with the open gates still stands. "The Spirit and the bride say, 'Come!' And let him who hears say, 'Come!' Whoever is thirsty, let him come; and whoever wishes, let him take the free gift of the water of life" (Rev. 22:17).

1. *The Revelation of St. John the Divine* (New York: Harper and Row, 1966), 261, 262.
2. *The Interpretation of Ezekiel in the Book of Revelation*, Ph.D. Diss., Harvard Univ., 1985 (Ann Arbor, Mich.: University Microfilms, Inc., 1987), 66-72.
3. "The Twelve Jewels of Rev. 21:19-20," *Journal of Biblical Literature* 100:3 (1981), 456.
4. Documented in G. K. Beale, *The Book of Revelation*, New International Greek Testament Commentary (Grand Rapids, Mich.: Eerdmans, 1999), 1057.
5. Ibid.

COSMIC SIGNS IN THE BOOK OF REVELATION

We may consider the book of Revelation an enlargement of Jesus' prophetic speech in the Gospels (Matthew 24, Mark 13, Luke 21). In these books, cosmic signs introduce Jesus' second coming. The Apocalypse expands upon these signs in two prophetic series: the seals (Rev. 6) and the last plagues (Rev. 16). This is evident when we compare the cosmic signs in all three narratives:

Matthew 24:29, 30 (NASB)	Revelation 6:12-14 (NASB)	Revelation 16:18-20 (NASB)
Immediately after the tribulation of those days the sun will be darkened, and the moon will not give its light, and the stars will fall from the sky, and the powers of the heavens will be shaken, and	I looked when He broke the sixth seal, and there was a great earthquake [Greek: *seismos megas*]; and the sun became black . . . and the whole moon became like blood; and the stars of	There were flashes of lightning . . . and peals of thunder; and there was a great earthquake [Greek: *seismos megas*], such as there had not been since man came to be upon the earth, so

159

Matthew 24:29, 30 (NASB)	Revelation 6:12-14 (NASB)	Revelation 16:18-20 (NASB)
then the sign of the Son of Man will appear in the sky.	the sky fell to the earth. . . . And the sky was split apart like a scroll when it is rolled up; and every mountain and island were moved out of their places.	great [*megas*] an earthquake was it and so mighty. . . . And every island fled away, and the mountains were not found.

All three accounts describe cosmic signs as the introduction to the Second Coming, or Judgment Day.

To make the correct historical application of the cosmic signs, we must note their connection with the time of tribulation that Matthew 24 describes; the signs follow "immediately after" that tribulation (Matt. 24:29). Some Bible students have not noticed that this unequaled "great tribulation" [Greek: *thlipsis megalê*] of Matthew 24:21 refers directly to the unequaled final distress of the saints in Daniel 12:1 [Greek: *thlipsis*], as every Bible indicates in its margin. A comparison of the language of both passages clearly demonstrates this correspondence:

Daniel 12:1 (NASB)	Matthew 24:21, 22 (NASB)
At that time [see 11:40-45] Michael, the great prince who stands guard over the sons of your people, will arise. And *there will be a time of distress* [Greek: *thlipsis*] *such as never occurred since there was a nation until that time;* and at that time your people, everyone who is found written in the book, will be rescued.	Then *there will be a great tribulation* [Greek: *thlipsis*], *such as has not occurred since the beginning of the world until now, nor ever shall.* And unless those days had been cut short, no life would have been saved; but for the sake of the elect those days shall be cut short.

Daniel provided the inspired chronology of salvation history upon which Jesus and the Apocalypse based their prophecies (see Matt.

24:15). So, Daniel's book is critical to understanding Jesus' prophecy in Matthew 24:29. Daniel speaks of more than one period of distress, but he locates the final tribulation in "the appointed time of the end" (Dan. 8:19; cf. 11:40; 12:1). Jesus knew, of course, about the three and a half "times" of distress that would come during the Middle Ages (Dan. 7:25) and about the global distress at the end of the age (in Dan. 12:1). What He referred to in Matthew 24:21, 29 in answer to the disciples' question about the end was not a "distress" limited to Daniel 7:25's three and a half "times" of persecution. As the table above shows, He clearly alluded to the end-time distress of Daniel 12:1. So, the cosmic signs, which Jesus said would come "immediately after the tribulation of those days," must come *after* the end-time distress!

Revelation's series of seven seals and seven plagues confirm this timing of the cosmic signs. And both prophetic chains add a "great earthquake" to the cosmic signs that usher in "the great day" of the wrath of God (see Rev. 6:12, 17; 16:18-20), a sign not mentioned in Jesus' prophetic speech of Matthew 24. A brief review of the evidence will place this cosmic quake in the proper perspective.

The Cosmic Earthquake in the Prophetic Outlook

Scripture often speaks of creation shaking before God's coming as Warrior to lead His hosts in the battle against His enemies (see Judg. 5:4, 5; Joel 2:10, 11; Mic. 1:3, 4; Ps. 18:7-9). And in many Old Testament prophecies, a worldwide earthquake accompanies a theophany (appearance) of the Creator of heaven and earth. Nahum's description of the coming of God to judge the world is representative: "The mountains quake before him and the hills melt away. The earth trembles at his presence, the world and all who live in it" (Nah. 1:5). Other prophets also portray God's coming as accompanied by a shaking of the heavens and earth:

I shall make the heavens tremble, and the earth will be shaken from its place, at the fury of the LORD of hosts in the day of His burning anger (Isa. 13:13, NASB; see also 24:18-20).

All the host of heaven will wear away, and the sky will be rolled up like a scroll; all their hosts will also wither away as a leaf withers from the vine, or as one withers from the fig tree (Isa. 34:4, NASB; see also Ezek. 38:20).

Thus says the Lord of hosts, "Once more in a little while, I am going to shake the heavens and the earth, the sea also and the dry land. And I will shake all the nations" (Hag. 2:6, 7 NASB).

This cosmic quake reminds us of God's first appearance on Mount Sinai, when "the whole mountain quaked violently" (Exod. 19:18, NASB). The connection identifies the Redeemer-King of Israel as the Judge of all the earth. Richard Bauckham rightly sees this prophetic perspective as the climax of prophecy: "The identifications of the eschatological theophany as a new Sinai theophany belongs to the apocalyptists' understanding of salvation-history, whereby God's redemptive acts in the future are portrayed on the model of his past acts."[1] Revelation explains that God will cause the cosmic quake when He speaks the words, "It is done" (see chap. 16:17, 18). It adds as another cause God's appearing as the Judge: "Earth and sky fled from his presence, and there was no place for them" (20:11).

In the light of the biblical perspective described above, we may understand the sixth seal (Rev. 6:12-17) as the fulfillment of the predicted shaking of the heavens and earth. The first five seals disclose the urgent need of the sixth seal. They portray sufferings and deaths of the saints during the long centuries an apostate church has oppressed them. In the fifth seal the martyrs ask this fundamental question: " 'How long, Sovereign Lord, holy and true, until you judge the inhabitants of the earth and avenge our blood?' " (v. 10). After acknowledging the righteousness of their cause, God counsels them "to wait a little longer," until the saints have endured the final distress (v. 11). The martyrs' plea will finally be answered in the sixth seal. "A great earthquake," combined with the shaking of all the heavenly bodies, marks the opening of this seal (vs. 12-14).

Some have questioned whether the sixth seal depicts the inauguration of the judgment at the Second Coming. They suggest that Revelation 6:12 merely announces a few isolated cosmic signs that precede that judgment, thus implying a further time of waiting for the martyrs during the sixth seal. This assumption creates two different earthquakes in the sixth seal: a smaller one in Revelation 6:12 and the cosmic quake in verse 14. But there are serious exegetical problems with this view. To apply the cosmic signs to intermittent occurrences over hundreds of years disturbs the focus of the sixth seal on the fulfillment of the martyrs' request and disconnects the cosmic signs from the Creator's return. The question is, Does the sixth seal really predict two separate earthquakes and two separate shakings of the stars?

Two Earthquakes in the Sixth Seal?

The literary form of Revelation 6:12-17 seems to offer a satisfactory answer to our question. Here's the entire passage:

> [12]And I looked when He broke the sixth seal, and there was a great earthquake; and the sun became black as sackcloth made of hair, and the whole moon became like blood; [13]and the stars of the sky fell to the earth, as a fig tree casts its unripe figs when shaken by a great wind. [14]And the sky was split apart like a scroll when it is rolled up; and every mountain and island were moved out of their places.
>
> [15]And the kings of the earth and the great men and the commanders and the rich and the strong and every slave and free man, hid themselves in the caves and among the rocks of the mountains; [16]and they said to the mountains and to the rocks, "Fall on us and hide us from the presence of Him who sits on the throne, and from the wrath of the Lamb; [17]for the great day of their wrath has come; and who is able to stand?" (NASB)

There is no biblical reason to interpret this seal as a chronological sequence of cosmic upheavals that occur over a period of hundreds of years. No previous seal has intermittent fulfillments; they all portray continuous events. In the sixth seal, verses 12-14 describe the cosmic calamities on earth and in the sky and verses 15-17 portray their effects on people around the world. This suggests that the cosmic signs in verses 12-14 form a close-knit, indivisible unit that is followed by a description of the impact of these signs on a single generation (vs. 15-17).

The structure John has given the passage—inverse parallelism—underlines the unity of verses 12-14:

A There is a great earthquake
  B The sun, moon, and stars are convulsed
  B' The sky recedes like a scroll rolling up
A' Every mountain and island is removed

The composition of the text indicates it is describing one and the same cosmic event—the shaking of heaven and earth—and not events separated by hundreds of years and affecting different generations. Lines A and A' parallel each other, and so do lines B and B'. Bible writers frequently used this parallelism. It isn't intended to describe two different events, but to emphasize and clarify a single event! So, the structure of verses 12-14 supports the view that there will be one great earthquake that will shake a single generation of people (6:15-17).

This interpretation is endorsed by the enlargement of the sixth seal in the seventh plague (Rev. 16:17-21), where the "great earthquake" is described again—this time in greater detail. Note the following comparison (from the NASB):

The Sixth Seal: Revelation 6:12-14 (NASB)	The Seventh Plague: Revelation 16:18-20 (NASB)
There was a great [Greek: *megas*] earthquake, . . . and every mountain and island were moved out of their places. And [all evildoers] . . .	Then there were flashes of lightning and . . . peals of thunder; and there was a great [Greek: *megas*] earthquake, such as there

The Sixth Seal: Revelation 6:12-14 (NASB)	The Seventh Plague: Revelation 16:18-20 (NASB)
said to the mountains and to the rocks, "Fall on us and hide us from the presence of Him who sits on the throne, and from the wrath of the Lamb; for the great day of their wrath has come; and who is able to stand?"	had not been since man came to be upon the earth, so great an earthquake was it, and so mighty. And the great city [Babylon] was split into three parts . . . And every island fled away, and the mountains were not found.

A comparison of the sixth seal and the seventh plague offers insights important to the interpretation of the sixth seal. The clause "there was a great earthquake" in 6:12 is repeated exactly in 16:18, where the final destruction of the cosmos is pictured. (The clauses are also exactly the same in the Greek original.) The passages' descriptions of the earthquakes' effects on earth and humankind resemble each other, except that the effects under the seventh plague are more extensive (see Rev. 16:17-21). So, any effort to distinguish between these two quakes grows out of something other than biblical exegesis.

The Cosmic Signs as Unique Events

The historicist application of the cosmic signs in Matthew 24 and Revelation 6 to past or contemporary history has not been unanimous or consistent. For instance, the Baptist William Miller argued strongly in 1840 that the sixth seal symbolically portrayed the French Revolution of 1789 and its aftermath.[2] Other historicists applied the cosmic signs of Revelation 6:12 literally to some of the contemporary natural upheavals, such as the Lisbon earthquake of November 1, 1755.[3] These reactions to that natural disaster were sincere responses that led multitudes to repentance and to a new interest in Bible prophecy. However, the modern science of seismology informs us that the Lisbon quake has often been surpassed in terms of intensity and deaths caused both prior to and after its occurrence.[4]

Similarly, when, on the night of November 13, 1833, a spectacular meteor shower struck fear in many hearts and bewildered the scientists of that time, people interpreted this event as the fulfillment of Bible prophecy. But ancient records have been found that report outstanding Leonid meteor storms in A.D. 902 (known as "the year of the stars") and in 1202, 1366, 1533, 1766, and 1799. Because of these records, Sir Isaac Newton calculated that the Leonids might return in 1866, which they did. The *Guinness Book of Records* of 1992 reports: "The greatest shower on record occurred on the night of 16-17 Nov. 1966, when the Leonid meteors (which recur every 33 1/3 years) were visible between North America and eastern USSR."[5]

So, we must face the question: Can we isolate a few instances from these groups of natural upheavals and call them signs of the end in the sense of unique fulfillments of Bible prophecies (Matt. 24:29; Rev. 6:12)? Or should we view such phenomena as partial fulfillments that remind us of prophecy's ultimate intention in specifying cosmic signs?

Those who seek support for a historical application connect the cosmic signs with Revelation 12:6's prophecy of 1260 days of religious persecution (A.D. 538-1798). On this basis, one author asserts: "Geography, sequence, and timing make this series of events [starting with the Lisbon quake] unique and unmatched by any earthquakes or meteor showers elsewhere or at other times."[6] Another claims: "The series of signs [Matt. 24:29] that were to take place 'immediately after the tribulation of those days' has evidently been fulfilled."[7] Their conclusion is based on a combination of two prophetic passages:

"But immediately after the tribulation of *those days,* the sun will be darkened, and the moon will not give its light, and the stars will fall from the sky, and the powers of the heavens will be shaken" (Matt. 24:29, NASB).

And the woman fled into the wilderness where she had a place prepared by God, so that there she might be nourished for *one thousand two hundred and sixty days* (Rev. 12:6, NASB).

However, a close look at the contexts of the two passages reveals that the periods referred to by the "those days" in Matthew 24:29

and the 1,260 days in Revelation 12:6 are not identical. In the first place, the book of Revelation was written long after the Gospels were written, so Matthew 24 does not presuppose Revelation 12 but rather the book of Daniel. Secondly, there is not the slightest hint in Matthew 24 that restricts the "days" of the unequaled "great tribulation" (in verses 21, 22, 29) to 1,260 years or to the Middle Ages, as if Jesus forgot to mention the days of the final tribulation Daniel 12:1 foretold. Indeed, Jesus undoubtedly included the days of final distress, as can be seen in His verbal allusion to Daniel 12:1 in Matthew 24:21 (see parallel columns above).

However, basing his approach on Daniel 7:25 and 12:1, John *did* distinguish clearly between two major periods of religious persecution—see Revelation 12:6, 17. His book dwells increasingly on the second period, the final distress of the saints (see chapters 13:15-17; 17:12-14; 19:11-21). This evidence should prevent us from over-looking the full scope of Jesus' forecast of the unequaled "great distress" that will be followed "immediately" by the cosmic signs that introduce and accompany His glorious coming. Jesus' divine intervention through the seven last plagues (Rev. 16–17) will shorten the final tribulation. Only the last plagues bring the shaking of the heavens and the earth (16:8-10, 17-21).

Some contemporary Adventist expositors frankly admit the exegetical problems with the traditional interpretation of the cosmic signs and turn their focus of attention away from any isolated event as a sign of the end. One leading evangelist wisely counseled:

If we are looking for specific events to indicate the nearness of Christ's return we will either misinterpret events and try to squeeze current events into prophecy, or we will be disappointed looking for an event that doesn't transpire. But if we look at trends we will see an increasingly clear Bible scenario of the coming of Jesus.[8]

The New Testament scholar Jon Paulien explains the signs of the times in Matthew 24 in accordance with the context and boldly declares:

The famines, pestilences, earthquakes, wars, and rumors of wars are not listed as signs of the end in Matthew 24. Instead they are "signs of the age," events that would occur throughout the interim between Jesus' earthly ministry and the end. Jesus did not want those who observe such events to calculate their significance for the timing of the end. Instead, He wanted those who observe wars, earthquakes, and famines to *keep watch.*[9]

The cosmic signs in the book of Revelation are not given to offer another opportunity to repent, but as a warning that it will be too late for repentance when the shaking of the heavens and the earth begins. The sixth seal provides a graphic demonstration of this. When the cosmic signs *begin* to occur, the people then living fully realize that their day of grace has ended. They cry, " 'The great day of their wrath has come, and who can stand?' " (Rev. 6:17). So, the gospel presses home the urgent message: "Now is the time of God's favor, now is the day of salvation" (2 Cor. 6:2). If we apply this truth to our hearts daily, we will be able to stand in the day of the cosmic signs.

---

1. R. Bauckham, *The Climax of Prophecy* (Edinburgh: Clark, 1993), 201.
2. *Evidence from Scripture and History of the Second Coming of Christ About the Year 1843* (Boston: B. Mussey, 1840), 184.
3. L. E. Froom, *The Prophetic Faith of Our Fathers* (Hagerstown, Md.: Review & Herald, 1954), Vol. 4:13.
4. See the *Encyclopedia Britannica Micropaedia,* 14th ed., (1997), Vol. 4:323, for a comprehensive listing.
4. Froom, ibid., Appendix B, "The Falling of the Stars."
5. New York: Facts on File, Inc.; D. McFarlan, ed., (1991), 12.
6. W. H. Shea, *Ministry,* Feb. 1999, 11.
7. C. M. Maxwell, *God Cares* (Nampa, Id.: Pacific Press, 1985), Vol. 2:202.
8. Mark Finley, *Adventists Affirm,* Vol. 6:1 (1992), 13.
9. Jon Paulien, *What the Bible Says About the End Time* (Hagerstown, Md.: Review & Herald, 1994), 157. See also G. R. Knight, *Matthew,* The Abundant Life Bible Amplifier (Nampa, Id.: Pacific Press, 1994), 236, 237; H. LaRondelle, "The Application of Cosmic Signs in the Adventist Tradition," *Ministry,* Sept. 1998, 25-27.

Appendix B

"THIS GENERATION WILL CERTAINLY NOT PASS AWAY"*

Jesus announced that in the end times cosmic events would take place with such dramatic effect that " 'the heavenly bodies will be shaken' " (Matt. 24:29; Mark 13:24; Luke 21:25). After these events " 'the sign of the Son of Man will appear in the sky. . . . They will see the Son of Man coming on the clouds of the sky, with power and great glory' " (Matt. 24:30). Jesus wanted His followers to look for that "sign of the Son of Man"!

In connection with these signs of His return, Jesus gave this parable:

"Learn this lesson from the fig tree: As soon as its twigs get tender and its leaves come out, you know that summer is near. Even so, when you see all these things [Greek: *tauta*], you know that it [or "he"] is near, right at the door. I tell you

*The basic content of this appendix was first published in the September 1999, *Ministry* magazine. It is used here by permission of *Ministry's* editor.

the truth, *this generation* will certainly not pass away until *all these things* [Greek: *panta tauta*] have happened" (Matt. 24:32-34).

Some theologians have concluded that in these comments Jesus was announcing that He would return during the lifetime of the generation then living. The Parousia, they say, should have taken place shortly after the destruction of Jerusalem in A.D. 70; history has shown that Jesus was simply mistaken.

Is their claim correct?

To understand Jesus' statement adequately, we must consider two crucial terms: "this generation" and "all these things." Understanding the latter phrase is crucial to understanding the former.

What then did Jesus mean by "*all* these things"?

Luke's apocalyptic material resembles that of Matthew's quoted above. He mentions "signs in the sun, moon and stars," seismic waves in the sea, and then summarizes: "the heavenly bodies will be shaken" (21:25, 26). And after his version of the fig-tree parable, he also repeats the idea: " 'Even so, when you see these things [Greek: *tauta*] happening, you know that the kingdom of God is near' " (21:31). It is clear that "these things" do not include the Parousia itself. Obviously, it is pointless to say, "When you see the Son of Man coming in glory, you know that He is near."

So, both Matthew and Luke mention cosmic upheavals as the last sign before the coming of Jesus (Matt. 24:29). We can only conclude that the last generation has come when we've witnessed the occurrence of *all* these cosmic signs—not just the meteor shower of 1833.

At the 1952 SDA Bible Conference, Arthur S. Maxwell said that if the cosmic phenomena of the year 1833 were intended as a sign of the approach of the final consummation, "how absurd to suggest that hundreds of years may elapse before the Lord shall appear! Prolonged delay would make them meaningless."[1] At the same Bible conference, William H. Branson, president of the General Conference, declared, "Nowhere do we find a statement of Jesus that some of those who witnessed the falling of the stars [of Nov. 13, 1833] would live until He appears. He says of those who are to constitute the last generation, 'When we shall see *all* these things,' and I want to ask which generation it is that saw *all* these things come to pass? That really is the crux of the question."[2]

The question is answered when we relate Jesus' statement of "this generation" to the last sign of the "shaking of the heavenly bodies" and relate the latter to the cosmic events that will occur during the seven last plagues. In fact, most Bible scholars hold that the clause "the heavenly bodies will be shaken" (Matt. 24:29) simply summarizes the signs in the sun, moon, and stars. Present Adventist New Testament scholars teach this concept.[3]

The cosmic signs of Matthew 24:29, then, serve the purpose of introducing the Day of Jesus.

"This Generation" in Typological Perspective

What did Jesus mean by the term "this generation" [Greek: *hê genea hautê*] (Matt. 24:34)? Most commentators assume that Jesus was referring to His contemporary generation. They point to a similar statement that Jesus made: " 'I tell you the truth, all this will come upon this generation' " (Matt. 23:36). But the similarities do not prove that they mean the same thing—because the contexts differ. In chapter 23 Jesus was speaking about the imminent doom of Jerusalem (see verses 32, 35-38). In chapter 24 He was speaking about His second coming in glory (see verses 30, 31).

Jesus did not indicate how long the period of His contemporary generation would last. To that generation of unbelievers, He made the startling announcement: " 'You will not see me again until you say, "Blessed is he who comes in the name of the Lord" ' " (Matt. 23:39). Jesus announced the same truth to the high priest Caiaphas: " 'From now on [Greek: *ap' arti*] *you* will see the Son of Man seated at the right hand of Power and coming on the clouds of heaven' " (Matt 26:64, NRSV; NASB margin; cf. Luke 22:69; Mark 14:62).

This prediction necessitates the resurrection of Caiaphas at

Jesus' second advent. The book of Revelation speaks of just such a resurrection: "He is coming with the clouds, and every eye will see him, *even those who pierced him;* and all the peoples of the earth will mourn because of him" (Rev. 1:7).

In part, Jesus meant His statement that "this generation shall not pass away" to apply to all His major opponents in every generation. They will all be resurrected at His second advent and face Him as their Judge. Jesus' point was not the chronological life span of "this generation" but His sure coming in judgment for His contemporary generation and for all who have "pierced Him" with their rejection.

Regarding the coming destruction of Jerusalem and its temple, Jesus said that it would take place during His contemporary generation (Matt. 23:36). They were to experience the " 'time of punishment in fulfillment of all that has been written' " (Luke 21:22). This judgment serves also as a prophetic type of the last judgment, when " 'all the nations of the earth will mourn' " because of Jesus (Matt. 24:30; Rev. 1:7). Jesus' own generation thus functions as a type of the last generation that will reject His Messiahship.

The disciples' questions concerned the timing of His second coming as well (Matt. 24:3). But Jesus never declared that He would return during the lifetime of the existing generation. Of His Parousia He said, " 'No one knows that day or hour, not even the angels in heaven, nor the Son, but only the Father. Be on guard! Be alert! You do not know when that time will come' " (Mark 13:32, 33).

The Theological Connotation of "This Generation"

Some propose that Jesus' phrase "this generation" refers to all who are at any time classified as "this adulterous and sinful generation" or "unbelieving generation" because they reject the gospel message. C. Mervyn Maxwell preferred this interpretation because the temporal understanding of "generation" as people who were alive at the time of the events of 1833 no longer makes sense: none of them are still alive.[4]

Jesus indeed frequently equates the phrase "this generation" with an unbelieving generation (see Mark 9:19; Matt. 12:39; 17:17). He connected the faithless attitude of His own generation directly with that of those who suffer the final judgment when He stated:

"The men of Nineveh will stand up at the judgment with this generation, and condemn it" (Matt. 12:41).

"For whoever is ashamed of Me and My words in this adulterous and sinful generation, of him the Son of Man also will be ashamed when He comes in the glory of His Father with the holy angels" (Mark 8:38, NKJV).

Jesus used the phrase "this generation" to designate a generation that has been confronted with His truth and has, for the most part, rejected His Lordship.

But are there any indications that Jesus had specifically the final generation in mind when He said, " 'This generation will not pass away' "? Some references in His Olivet discourse clearly point to the final generation:

1. Jesus' phrase " 'there will be great distress, unequaled from the beginning of the world until now' " (Matt. 24:21; see Mark 13:19 for a variation) has a specific end-time ring. This phrase resembles the one in Daniel 12:1 that describes the last generation of saints.

Equally compelling is Jesus' prediction:

"Immediately after the distress of those days [of Dan. 12:1!] 'the sun will be darkened, and the moon will not give its light; the stars will fall from the sky, and the heavenly bodies will be shaken' " (Matt. 24:29).

This chronological pinpointing of "all these things" in the sky "immediately after the distress"[5] can find its complete fulfillment only in the generation that experiences the end-time distress or "time of Jacob's trouble" (Jer. 30:5-7; Gen. 32:23-26) of Daniel

12:1. This will take place during the seven last plagues that cause the cosmic upheavals and directly usher in the Second Advent (Rev. 16:10, 17-21).[6]

2. Luke's Gospel presents the cosmic signs as an unbreakable unit that introduces Jesus' return to the last generation:

" 'There will be signs in the sun, moon, and stars. On the earth, nations will be in anguish and perplexity at the roaring and tossing of the sea. Men will faint from terror, apprehensive of what is coming on the world, for the heavenly bodies will be shaken. At that time they will see the Son of Man coming in a cloud with power and great glory. When these things begin to take place, stand up and lift up your heads, because your redemption is drawing near' " (Luke 21:25-28).

3. Looking at the larger textual unit, Matthew 23–25, one can discern a broad chiastic structure (23:1–24:14 paralleling 24:15–25:46) in which the phrase "this generation" occurs twice (23:36; 24:34). Discussing this literary structure, S. J. Kidder states: "The first 'generation' was to witness the signs on earth, the second was to witness the signs in heaven."[7] This means that just as the unbelieving generation of Jesus' time saw the sign of Jerusalem's destruction (23:36), so the unbelieving generation of the end time will see the sign of Jesus' coming on the clouds of heaven (24:34).

Jesus foresaw the generation that will live at "the end" of time.* The last wicked generation in the church age will experience God's final "wrath" in the seven last plagues that culminate in the shaking of heaven and earth (Rev. 16:10, 17-21). It will certainly not pass away before it sees Jesus' advent as the Judge and Deliverer.

The sixth seal contains a description of the effect of these terrifying events on the world:

I watched as he opened the sixth seal. There was a great earth-

---

*The phrase "the end" (Greek: *to telos* or *hê synteleia*) is similar to the one Daniel used; Jesus used it repeatedly of the end of the church age (Matt. 10:22; 13:39; 24:3, 13, 14; 28:20).

quake. The sun turned black like sackcloth made of goat hair, the whole moon turned blood red, and the stars in the sky fell to earth, as late figs drop from a fig tree when shaken by a strong wind. The sky receded like a scroll, rolling up, and every mountain and island was removed from its place.

Then the kings of the earth, the princes, the generals, the rich, the mighty, and every slave and every free man hid in caves and among the rocks of the mountains. They called to the mountains and the rocks, "Fall on us and hide us from the face of him who sits on the throne and from the wrath of the Lamb! For the great day of their wrath has come, and who can stand?" (Rev. 6:12-17).

Evidently, the sixth seal portrays the last generation on earth and its experience of the shaking of heaven and earth. That generation alone will see the "all things" that Jesus predicted. It is the generation that is alive when the seven last plagues fall on the Babylonish world when it attempts to destroy the followers of Jesus (see Rev. 17:14: 19:11-21).

Jesus assigned all His followers the duty of watching for the fulfillment of the signs of the times, especially of the supreme sign of all: the coming of the Son of Man *on a cloud of glory*. They were never to think that His return might be far off in time because no one knows when it will take place. He will arrive suddenly and unexpectedly (Mark 13:32; Matt. 24:36). In every generation, Jesus' disciples must cultivate an expectant attitude: " 'What I say to you, I say to everyone: "Watch!" ' " (Mark 13:37).

The first-century Christians saw some of the signs of the age fulfilled before their eyes, so they anticipated the end with intensified hope. Many believers during the Middle Ages experienced the predicted signs of apostasy, great distress, and horrible persecution. During the Advent awakening in the nineteenth century, many interpreted the natural upheavals on earth and in the sky that they saw as forerunners of the Second Coming. How much the more do we need to be alert today and seek a better understanding of the prophecies of Jesus' coming! We may be the generation that will see all the signs fulfilled.

---

1. In *Our Firm Foundation* (Hagerstown, Md.: Review & Herald, 1953), Vol. 2:226.

2. Ibid., 701.

3. See Harold E. Fagal, *The Advent Hope in Scripture and History*, V. N. Olsen, ed. (Hagerstown, Md.: Review & Herald, 1987), 52.

4. See *God Cares* (Nampa, Id.: Pacific Press, 1985), Vol. 2:44.

5. For a discussion of "those days" in Matt. 24:29, see H. LaRondelle, "The Application of Cosmic Signs in the Adventist Tradition," *Ministry*, Sept. 1998, 25-27. See also his *How to Understand the End-time Prophecies* (Sarasota, Fl.: First Impressions, 1997), chap. 6.

6. See the interpretation of Dan. 12:1 by E. G. White in *The Great Controversy* (Nampa, Id.: Pacific Press, 1950), chap. 39, "The Time of Trouble"; see esp. pp. 616-621.

7. S. J. Kidder, " 'This Generation' in Matthew 24:34," *Andrews University Seminary Studies*, Vol. 21:3 (1983), 205.

Appendix C

THE ABIDING HALLMARK
OF THE
TRUE CHURCH*

John's Apocalypse states repeatedly that a twofold tenet of faith—"the Word of God and the testimony of Jesus" (with some variations)—characterizes Jesus' true church (see Rev. 1:2, 9; 6:9; 12:17; 14:12; 20:4). This twofold description functions as the divine standard that defines the Christian's faithfulness to God. The application of these texts in Revelation covers the entire Christian era.

We can see a basic parallel of this hallmark of the church in Isaiah's test of truth: "To the law and to the testimony! If they do not speak according to this word, they have no light of dawn" (Isa. 8:20). This twofold standard represented the final authority within Israel, "Moses and the prophets" (see 2 Kings 17:13). Jesus referred to this twofold authority in Matthew 5:17, " 'Do not think that I have come to abolish the Law or the Prophets,' " and again

---

*This appendix is a revision of pages 281-290 of my book *How to Understand the End-Time Prophecies of the Bible* (Sarasota, Fl.: First Impressions, 1997).

in His parable of the rich man and Lazarus: "Abraham replied, 'They have Moses and the Prophets; let them listen to them' " (Luke 16:29, see also 24:27). And Paul summed up the Old Testament as "the Law and the Prophets" (Rom. 3:21). These two constituent parts of the Hebrew Bible formed the canonical norm used to determine true worship in ancient Israel. (The unity of the Hebrew Scriptures made it possible for them to be referred to in a single term: *the Law* [in Hebrew: *Torah*]. For example, on one occasion, Jesus, when citing from a psalm, asked: " 'Is it not written *in your Law,* "I have said you are gods"?' " [John 10:34; Psalm 82:6].)

However, Jesus claimed that His testimony *expanded* the canon of divine authority: " 'There is a judge for the one who rejects me and does not accept *my words;* that very word which I spoke will condemn him at the last day' " (John 12:48). Jesus explained His authority this way: " 'The one who comes from above is above all. He testifies to what he has seen and heard, but no one accepts his testimony' " (John 3:31, 32). The New Testament proclaims Jesus' testimony as the extended Word of God:

> In the past God spoke to our forefathers through the prophets at many times and in various ways, but in these last days he has spoken to us by his Son, whom he appointed heir of all things, and through whom he made the universe (Heb.1:1, 2).

The testimony of Jesus was the Word of God, for God gave Jesus His Spirit "without limit" (John 3:34; see Isa. 42:1). Jesus possessed the Spirit of prophecy in divine fullness. The apostolic church accepted Jesus' testimony as the final authority for interpreting the Law and the Prophets. This testimony of Jesus is incorporated in the four Gospels, and interpreted in the inspired epistles of the New Testament.

It was the apostle Paul who gave the phrase "the testimony [Greek: *to martyrion*] of Jesus" its definitive gospel meaning. He wrote to the church of Corinth that "the testimony of Jesus was confirmed" among them as evidenced by their many gifts of the Spirit (1 Cor. 1:6, NKJV). Paul used the phrase "the testimony of Jesus" in the sense of the gospel, the proclaimed message of salvation in Jesus. For Paul the "testimony of Jesus" was equal to "the testimony of God" (1 Cor. 2:1). He was not ashamed to die for "the testimony of our Lord" (2 Tim. 1:8 NKJV).

John wrote that he was on the island of Patmos "because of the word of God and the testimony of Jesus" (Rev. 1:9). Exegetical scholars (for instance, I. T. Beckwith, H. B. Swete, L. A. Vos, R. H. Mounce, G. B. Caird, A. A. Trites, and G. R. Beasley Murray) understand the genitive expressions "of God" and "of Jesus" in Revelation 1:2, 9 as subjective genitives—that is, God spoke the word and Jesus gave the testimony that John wrote of in these verses. We may conclude, then, that God's progressive revelation places the church under the authority of His Son (see Heb. 1:1, 2; 2:1-4; 10:26-31; 12:22-29).

Jesus' Testimony for the Churches

The book of Revelation was intended to prepare the church for severe persecution. A great number of believers were to be brought before courts and condemned, some even to death. For this reason Jesus encouraged them to *hold to* the "testimony of Jesus" just as He had witnessed faithfully before Pontius Pilate (1 Tim. 6:12-14; Rev. 1:5, 9; 2:25; 3:11; 5:9; 12:11, 17). The "apocalypse of Jesus Christ" (Rev. 1:2) itself became a constitutive part of Jesus' witness; it is His "testimony for the churches" (22:16; 1:2). For this "testimony of Jesus" John suffered on Patmos (1:9) and countless martyrs sacrificed their lives in the course of history (6:9). It is also this "testimony of Jesus" that the remnant church will "have" or "hold to" during the final conflict with the antichrist (12:17), even when they are threatened with death (13:15-17).

So, it is not only the end-time church who may "have" the testimony of Jesus; "the testimony of Jesus" has abiding validity for the

Revelation 1:9	Revelation 6:9	Revelation 12:17
I, John, . . . was on the island of Patmos because of *the word of God and the testimony of Jesus.*	When he opened the fifth seal, I saw . . . those who had been slain because of *the word of God and the testimony they maintained* [Greek: *eichon*— "had," "held," "possessed," "preserved"].	The dragon . . . went off to make war against the rest of her offspring—those who *obey God's commandments and hold to* [Greek: *echonton*— "have," "hold," "possess," "preserve"] *the testimony of Jesus.*

church of the ages. In fact, this testimony is the essential hallmark of Jesus' followers during the *entire* Christian age. This can be seen in the following overview:

Revelation 1:9 and 6:9 provide the primary guidelines for interpreting the hallmark of the remnant church given in Revelation 12:17. The "word of God and testimony of Jesus" is "the faith . . . once for all entrusted to the saints" (see Jude 3). One must have endurance to "hold fast to the faith of Jesus" (Rev. 14:12, NRSV). In the final conflict of the ages, God calls His church to stand firm on His everlasting law and gospel in continuity with the church of the apostles and martyrs (see 14:6). The end-time church will be known by her faithfulness to the biblical commandments of God and to the biblical testimony of Jesus (12:17). In this way the end-time people of God demonstrate the true apostolic succession.

"The testimony" that Revelation 6:9 says the martyrs "had" parallels "the testimony of Jesus" that chapter 12:17 says the remnant people of God "have." People usually overlook this important parallel. The verb "to have" [Greek: *echein*] in these two passages is the same and so, of course, must have the same meaning—which can also include the idea "to keep, to preserve, to hold fast" (see, e.g., Paul's use of this verb in 1 Tim. 3:9; 2 Tim. 1:13).[1] Several scholars—among them Beckwith, Swete, Caird, and Mounce—have argued persuasively that the "testimony" that the martyrs of the church age had (Rev. 6:9) is identical with "the testimony of Jesus" mentioned elsewhere in the Revelation (1:9; 12:17; 19:10; 20:4). Gerhard Pfandl applies this to Revelation 6:9, stating:

> We concur with Mounce who says the martyrs' testimony was not primarily their witness about Jesus but the witness that they had received from him (cf. 12:17; 20:4). They had accepted it, they refused to give it up, and consequently, they were put to death. The "testimony", no less than the "word", was an objective possession of the martyrs.[2]

The Testimony for Which the Martyrs Died

The crucial question is, For what kind of "objective" testimony of Jesus were the martyrs willing to lay down their lives? One scholar identifies it as "a deposit of teachings from the Lord, commandments and teachings which have specific content and form so they can be kept and held!"[3] The martyrs that Revelation 6:9 and 20:4 mention died primarily for the sake of the testimony Jesus gave and in a secondary sense for their witness to Jesus' testimony. That's true also of the final generation of God's people spoken of in Revelation 12:17. Beatrice S. Neall confirms this exegesis:

> "The word of God and the testimony of Jesus" must be understood as the gospel of Jesus' death and resurrection (Rev. 1:18), His power to save from sin (1:5; 12:10-11) and transform men into His likeness (14:1) through the blood of the Lamb (7:14; 12:11)[4]

Remarkably, Revelation 20:4 mentions faithfulness to "the testimony of Jesus" as the primary characteristic of the end-time martyrs:

> I saw the souls of those who had been beheaded because of their testimony for Jesus [literally: "because of the testimony of Jesus" NASB] *and because of the word of God.* They had not

worshiped the beast or his image and had not received his mark on their foreheads or their hands (Rev. 20:4).

It is in regard to the testimony of Jesus and the Word of God that the remnant church will be adjudged faithful to the "Lamb" in her battle with the "beast." The crisis this church faces does not differ essentially from the previous crises the book of Revelation describes. Kenneth A. Strand clarified the issue in several places:

> In the book of Revelation faithfulness to the "word of God" and to the "testimony of Jesus Christ" separates the faithful from the faithless, and it brings about persecution that includes John's own exile and the martyrdom of other believers (see again 1:9; 6:9; 12:17; 20:4; etc.).[5]
>
> The [Old Testament] witness and the apostolic testimony . . . carry a message that afforded abundant comfort and hope for the first-century Christians and have done so, as well, for all followers of Jesus ever since.[6]

The remnant people and their loyalty to Jesus are mentioned again in Revelation 14:12, which functions as an explanatory paral-

Revelation 12:17, NKJV	Revelation 14:12, NKJV
He [the dragon] went to make war with the rest of her offspring, *who keep the commandments of God and have the testimony of Jesus Christ.*	Here is the patience of the saints; here are those *who keep the commandments of God and the faith of Jesus.*

lel to Revelation 12:17:

The remnant people not only keep God's commandments but also keep the "faith of Jesus" (Rev. 14:12). This "faith of Jesus" which His followers "keep" is not simply their subjective faith in Jesus but the objective faith or teachings of Jesus, which the apostles taught and kept faithfully (Acts 2:42; 2 Tim. 4:7). Jude, the brother of James, urged the church "to contend for *the faith* that was once for all entrusted to the saints" (Jude 3, also v. 20). William G. Johnsson's comment on Revelation 14:12 is instructive:

> They keep the faith of Jesus. This expression does not mean that the people of God have faith *in* Jesus (although they do), because the faith of Jesus is something they *keep*. "The faith" probably refers to the Christian tradition, the body of teachings that center in Jesus. Jude 3 may provide a parallel: "the faith which was once for all delivered to the saints." When God's loyal followers keep the faith of Jesus they remain true to basic Christianity—they "keep the faith."[7]

The expression "the faith of Jesus" in Revelation 14:12 clarifies "the testimony of Jesus" in 12:17 and does not necessarily add a third characteristic of the remnant church. To "keep the faith of Jesus" implies to keep Jesus' teachings (see Rev. 3:8, 10; 22:7). It deserves mentioning that a small group of the followers of the Baptist preacher William Miller decided to associate themselves as a new denomination—*"taking the name, Seventh-day Adventists, covenanting to keep the commandments of God, and the faith of Jesus Christ."*[8] This event shows how influential the end-time prophecies of John's Apocalypse are. It also reveals what solemn obligation a denomination accepts in claiming to be the true church.

The Angel's Clarification

> At this I fell at his feet to worship him. But he said to me, "Do not do it! I am a fellow servant with you and with your brothers who hold to the testimony of Jesus. Worship God! For the testimony of Jesus is the spirit of prophecy" (Rev. 19:10).

We must interpret each text in the light of its context. This approach serves as a safeguard against unconscious manipulation of a text or phrase. Because the expression "the testimony of Jesus" occurs twice in Revelation 19:10, this text has received special scrutiny and careful exegesis by some professional exegetes (Louis Vos, David Hill, Richard Bauckham, and others). A problem arises when the interpreter cuts the last sentence of Revelation 19:10 from its context and gives it a meaning that replaces the testimony of Jesus as recorded in the New Testament with the abiding gift of prophecy. Such an understanding would make the testimony of Jesus in Revelation 12:17 exclusively a gift of visions to some chosen believers in the end-time. This concept reduces the meaning of the testimony of Jesus in the book of Revelation.

The angel whose words John recorded in Revelation 19:10 did *not* intend to substitute the Spirit of prophecy for the historic testimony of Jesus—as if the New Testament was suddenly to be excluded or ignored. His last statement in that verse is not so much a definition as it is an explanation. It explains that the angel and John are fellow servants in so far as all prophets share the testimony of Jesus, because the testimony of Jesus is the spirit of prophecy. Richard Bauckham offers this helpful explanation:

> The divine Spirit who gives John the visionary experience in which he may receive revelation communicates not the teaching of an angel but the witness which Jesus bears. . . . The equivalent of the reference to "the witness of Jesus" in 19:10 is now found in the words of the epilogue, in which the angel disappears from view and Jesus testifies directly: "I, Jesus have sent my angel to you with this testimony for the churches."[9]

Jesus explained that the Spirit of truth " 'will not speak on his own; . . . He will bring glory to me by taking from what is mine and making it known to you' " (John 16:13, 14; see also 14:26). The Spirit of prophecy has accomplished this in the Scriptures of the New Testament, which convey the testimony of Jesus to the church with canonical authority. What the Spirit says is what Jesus says. The seven letters of Jesus make this point; all of them conclude with the words: " 'He who has an ear, let him hear what the Spirit says to the churches' " (Rev. 2:7, 11, etc.). The angel explained to John that when the Spirit inspires prophecy, its content and authority come from Jesus Himself (19:10). The Spirit of prophecy thus reveals the testimony of Jesus. All true prophets are " 'those who hold to the testimony of Jesus' " (19:10; compare 22:9).

Revelation 22:9 includes all church members among the group that holds the testimony of Jesus: " 'I am a fellow servant with you and with your brothers the prophets *and of all who keep the words of this book.'* " Revelation 6:9 and 12:17 also have in view this enlarged circle of all faithful Christians that "have" the testimony of Jesus. Bauckham draws this practical conclusion:

> This [Rev. 19:10; 22:9] is an acknowledgment that the role to which Revelation calls all Christians is, in essence, the same as that of prophets: bearing the witness of Jesus, remaining faithful in word and deed to the one true God and his righteousness.[10]

This responsibility that church members share does not deny the Spirit's freedom to bestow on chosen individuals the spiritual gift of prophecy (see 1 Cor. 12:7-11) for the edification of the church (1 Cor. 14:1, 4). The manifestation of the abiding gift of prophecy in the post-apostolic church is part of the extended fulfillment of Joel 2:28, 29.[11]

The angel teaches John, however, that the "testimony of Jesus" that already exists is the testing truth for John, for his fellow prophets, for the church, and for the angels of God (see also Rev. 22:9). This "testimony of Jesus" constitutes the ultimate norm for all Christian worship and manifestations of the gift of prophecy.[12] To hold faithfully to this canonical "testimony of Jesus" is the sacred duty of prophets and angels. Such is the teaching of the interpreting angel in Revelation 19:10.

At that time John was struggling with a growing wave of false prophets in the churches of Asia (Rev. 2:20; 1 John 4:1), some of whom were deceiving the believers in Thyatira with "deep secrets" (Rev. 2:24). So, the Lord reminded John that the Spirit of prophecy mediates "the testimony of Jesus." Beasley-Murray comments: "The burden of prophecy, therefore, is the testimony which Jesus bore."[13] Believers must test all messages from post-apostolic prophets by the canonical testimony of Jesus (see Rev. 22:18, 19; 1 Thess. 5:19-21; 2 Pet. 3:2, 15, 16; Matt. 24:24). That normative testimony of Jesus will unmask the deceptive claims of "the false prophet" in the time of the end (see Rev. 16:13; 19:20; 20:10).

The restoration of the *historic* commandments of God and of the *historic* testimony or faith of Jesus will characterize the remnant church of Revelation 12:17; 14:12. These two characteristics were the identifying hallmark of the apostolic church (Rev. 1:9) and of the post-apostolic saints (6:9). They also constitute the hallmark of the remnant church, on which God has been pleased to bestow again the gift of the Spirit of prophecy. It is, however, the biblical testimony of Jesus that, in the book of Revelation, draws the line of demarcation between the faithful and the unfaithful. We concur with the conclusion of Kenneth A. Strand that "the word of God" and "the testimony of Jesus" in the book of Revelation refer to "what we today would call the Old Testament prophetic message and the New Testament apostolic witness."[14]

---

1. See W. F. Arndt and F. W. Gingrich, *A Greek-English Lexicon of the New Testament and Other Early Christian Literature* (Chicago: University of Chicago Press, 1957), 332.

2. In *Symposium on Revelation,* Book II. Daniel and Revelation Commentary Series, F. B. Holbrook, ed. (Silver Spring, Md.: Review & Herald, 1992), Vol. 7:313.

3. L. A. Vos, *The Synoptic Traditions in the Apocalypse* (Kampen: Kok, 1965), 203.

4. Beatrice Neall, *The Concept of Character in the Apocalypse With Implications for Character Education* (Washington, D.C.: University Press of America, 1983), 158.

5. K. A. Strand, *Andrews University Seminary Studies* 19:2 (1981), 133.

6. In *Symposium on Revelation,* II:206.

7. W. Johnsson, ibid., 38, 39.

8. *The Review and Herald,* Oct. 8, 1861.

9. R. Bauckham, *The Climax of Prophecy* (Edinburgh: Clark, 1993), 134.

10. Bauckham, *The Theology of the Book of Revelation* (Cambridge: Cambridge University Press, 1994), 121.

11. See E. G. White, *The Great Controversy* (Nampa, Idaho: Pacific Press, 1951), ix-xii. See also A. G. Daniells, *The Abiding Gift of Prophecy* (Nampa, Idaho: Pacific Press, 1946).

12. See J. D. G. Dunn, in *The New International Dictionary of New Testament Theology,* Colin Brown, ed. (Grand Rapids, Mich.: Zondervan, 1978), Vol. 3:706.

13. *Revelation,* The New Century Bible Commentary (Grand Rapids, Mich.: Eerdmans, 1983), 182.

14. *Andrews University Seminary Studies,* 19 (1981), 134.

If you enjoyed this book, you'll enjoy these as well:

Last Day Events
Ellen G. White. A compilation of statements about the end of time taken from 65 sources—published books, manuscript collections, and material never before published.
0-8163-1073-4. Hardcover. US$12.99, Cdn$18.99

The Coming Great Calamity
Marvin Moore. Marvin Moore calls our attention to startling biblical predictions of coming events that will usher in the new world order. Find out how everything really can change in the twinkling of an eye.
0-8163-1354-7. Paperback. US$10.99, Cdn$15.99

The Shape of the Coming Crisis
Don Mansell. This book shows a sequence of end-time events based on the writings of Ellen G. White. It's in-depth study of the Spirit of Prophecy shows that end-time events are already beginning to happen. The author is a former associate secretary of the White Estate.
0-8163-1402-0. Paper. US$12.99, Cdn$18.99

Order from your ABC by calling **1-800-765-6955**, or get online and shop our virtual store at **www.adventistbookcenter.com**.
    Read a chapter from your favorite book
    Order online
    Sign up for email notices on new products